Surf When
You Can

Surf When You Can

Lessons in Life, Loyalty, and Leadership from a Maverick Navy Captain

CAPTAIN

Brett Crozier

USN (RET)

With Michael Vlessides

ATRIA PAPERBACK

New York • Amsterdam/Antwerp • London •
Toronto • Sydney/Melbourne • New Delhi

ATRIA
PAPERBACK

An Imprint of Simon & Schuster, LLC
1230 Avenue of the Americas
New York, NY 10020

First Atria Paperback edition April 2025

ATRIA PAPERBACK and colophon are trademarks of Simon & Schuster, LLC

Interior design by Dana Sloan

Manufactured in the United States of America

1   3   5   7   9   10   8   6   4   2

Library of Congress Cataloging-in-Publication Data is available.

ISBN 978-1-9821-9100-9
ISBN 978-1-9821-9101-6 (pbk)
ISBN 978-1-9821-9102-3 (ebook)

*To the men and women
I had the privilege to
sail, surf, and fly
with throughout my career.*

Contents

Prologue

The gangplank, or brow, that connects the USS *Theodore Roosevelt* aircraft carrier to dry land is seventy-five feet long. But as I took my first steps down the brow on the evening of April 3, 2020—the last time I would do so as captain of one of the largest, most powerful, and most celebrated ships in the US Navy—it seemed like it stretched for a mile.

Just a few days before, I had sent an email to my superiors expressing concern over a COVID-19 outbreak that we were experiencing on the ship. In that email—which I'd sent over one of the Navy's unclassified networks—I tried to convey enough of a sense of urgency to motivate those in power to take the necessary steps to protect the lives of the five thousand crew on board the *Theodore Roosevelt*. Fortunately, it worked. It also cost me my job.

Within days, the Navy seemed to have taken my advice to heart and secured vacant hotel rooms across the island of Guam to separate and quarantine the Sailors, an impossible task in the close quarters of the ship, or even on the base. Even so, 1,200 Sailors—nearly one in four members of the crew—tested positive for COVID, and one died. Without such swift and decisive action, I was convinced that hundreds—maybe thousands—more would have contracted the virus, perhaps with fatal consequences. It was clear I'd had to take action. Nevertheless, the Navy disagreed with my methods (my email was eventually leaked to the press) and fired me for doing what I thought was right.

In the weeks and months that followed, I was afforded some free time to reflect back on my thirty-year career in the Navy, and the experiences that had brought me to that fateful decision. In doing so, I realized that over the course of those three decades I had learned a series of valuable lessons, lessons that have as much to do with life as they do with military leadership.

The lessons themselves have stood the test of time. They are the messages we've been told throughout our lives by our parents, our mentors, our teachers: value relationships; choose kindness; seek balance; communicate fearlessly; stand up for what you believe in; accept responsibility for your actions. Yet it is my sincere hope that these lessons—colored by the experiences I've had as a helicopter pilot, combat fighter pilot, ship captain, and naval officer—will help serve as a reminder that sometimes life's simplest lessons can prove to be the most valuable.

CHAPTER 1

Never Turn Down Espresso

Shortly after earning my wings as a combat helicopter pilot in 1994, I was assigned to my first squadron, the Easyriders of HSL-37, based in Barbers Point, Hawaii. It was the perfect assignment for a twenty-something California boy, where the turquoise waters of the South Pacific formed the backdrop to powdery white-sand beaches that seemed to stretch forever.

I was one of six combat helicopter pilots from the squadron assigned to Detachment 7, a close-knit group of pilots, aircrew, and maintainers. Together, Det7, as we called ourselves, was assigned to the USS *Fletcher*, a 550-foot destroyer stationed at Pearl Harbor. We trained with the *Fletcher* for months, after which we joined the ship at sea for operations. During these deployments we would conduct various flights, including surveillance missions where we would circle the destroyer at a radius of approximately 150 miles, keeping a watchful eye out for potential hostile contact with any number of nefarious actors with unfriendly intentions, including rogue Iranian elements and pirates hell-bent on disrupting international shipping channels.

In December 1996, the *Fletcher* was deployed to the Persian Gulf (also known as the Arabian Gulf) as part of the embargo against Iraq following its invasion of Kuwait. More than six hundred miles long and surrounded by Iraq, Iran, Saudi Arabia, and the United Arab Emirates, the warm, shallow waters of the Persian Gulf are peppered with oil rigs and crisscrossed every day by thousands of ships transporting goods.

As part of the United Nations embargo, any goods entering or leaving Iraq had to be inspected and certified. The UN was particularly concerned about the potential for the Iraqis to be buying and selling weapons. The only permitted products were the necessities of life. The *Fletcher* was part of the international force responsible for these inspections. And with so many ships in the gulf at any time, the work was considerable.

Most of the time, the vessels we encountered had the proper documentation for their goods and were allowed to proceed with their business. But if they didn't, we had to commandeer the vessel and sail it to Abu Dhabi, in the United Arab Emirates, where UN officials were waiting. The process was far from straightforward. Piracy was commonplace in the Persian Gulf at the time (it still is), and the potential for encountering hostility was real.

So we took no chances. Every inspection boat we sent from the *Fletcher* was escorted by a chopper overhead, machine guns pointed over the side and trained on the cargo ship's crew, just in case. Eventually we had commandeered half a dozen ships this way and had to sail the makeshift flotilla to Abu Dhabi, while being escorted by the *Fletcher*.

With so many suspicious vessels in tow, the *Fletcher*'s captain asked for officer volunteers to take command of each one for the seventy-two-hour journey to Abu Dhabi. We would work in teams of three: the temporary captain, a boatswain's mate (also called a "bosun's" mate) armed with a shotgun, and an operations specialist to help navigate. I jumped at the chance, and was soon offered command of a ship that claimed to be carrying car tires. And while tires were not considered a prohibited item under the UN sanctions, the crew was unable to confirm their relevant UN authorization numbers, which drew suspicion from the *Fletcher*.

The ship I was assigned to was the *Manna*, a 150-foot cargo dhow, a wooden boat that is one of the most common ships on the high seas. Think of the dhow as the naval world's pickup truck. It's cheap, easy to operate, and versatile. Most dhows have a raised platform at the back that serves as the bridge and a cavernous space in the middle where cargo is stored. While dhows carry water and some food, the crews on these ships typically keep themselves fed by fishing for plentiful local species such as bream, hamour, and rays.

Before we left the *Fletcher*, Captain Phillip Greene briefed the teams that would take command of the ships that had yet to verify their cargo.

"They might be hostile, so have weapons ready at all times," he said. "Watch your backs because they likely have knives, too. And whatever you do, don't eat anything they offer you." Clearly, we were entering enemy territory.

The boat ride over was tense. I carried a 9mm pistol on my waist, as did my operations specialist, Petty Officer Tommy Jones. Our beefy bosun's mate, Petty Officer Mike Sun, was armed with a shotgun. Overhead, two choppers circled low, machine guns ready.

"If things go down," I said to Mike, "be careful where you shoot that shotgun."

The dhow's crew eyed us warily as we boarded. The deck was covered in long rows of fish drying in the intense Middle Eastern heat. With the crew's eyes boring holes into the backs of our skulls, we investigated the cargo. Sure enough, the hold was full of car tires. Mike, Tommy, and I immediately let out a collective sigh of relief and began to feel more comfortable. These men were not pirates or smugglers after all. In fact, they seemed remarkably similar to us: people just simply trying to earn a living to support their families back home. Nevertheless, our orders called for us to escort any ship lacking proper documentation back to Abu Dhabi for approval and release, regardless of how innocuous its cargo may have been.

If there were any lingering tensions between us, they quickly evaporated once we opened our food stores to the dhow's crew. They marveled at what we brought: foot-long turkey and cheese subs, soda, chocolate chip cookies. As we invited them to eat their fill, the atmosphere became friendly, almost jovial.

The captain of the dhow, a small, friendly man named Ismail who wore a long white robe and white pants, looked on in wonder.

"Sir," he said to me in a thick Pakistani accent, "this is not what I expected. You have made the men very happy."

"It's the least we can do after delaying your trip," I said.

Other than eating, though, there was little for the dhow's crew to do now that we had taken command of the ship. Entertainment suddenly became *very important*, and the men spent much of their time glued to a small TV/VCR combination on the bridge, where they watched Pakistani movies.

I happened to have a VHS copy of Eddie Murphy's *The Nutty Professor* in my cabin on the *Fletcher*. So the next time one of our boats came out with supplies, I had them bring it . . . in the name of international diplomacy, of course.

I gathered the crew, popped the movie in, and we all sat down to watch. Even though they didn't speak a word of English, the men were mesmerized, doubling over with laughter and clapping all the while. When it was over, someone hit the rewind button and we all watched *The Nutty Professor* all over again, three American Navy Sailors and approximately a dozen Pakistani sailors, brought together under the unlikeliest of circumstances.

I took in the scene, watching this unexpected gathering of Pakistani men—some of whom were in their fifties and sixties— giggling at *The Nutty Professor* while drinking Sprite and eating turkey-and-cheese subs. It struck me that no matter how different we seemed, we managed to find common ground. Over the course of those next three days we became more familiar with one another. I was particularly fond of Ismail, a dedicated family man who I learned sent all of his earnings back home to Pakistan.

With a day to go in our journey, though, the atmosphere suddenly changed. As we steamed southward one afternoon, approximately fifty miles off the Iranian coast, a number of boats appeared on the horizon. Each was manned by a crew of armed Iranians.

Ismail scowled. He didn't know much English, but he knew the word for these people.

"Pirates," he growled.

He explained to me that these Iranian bandits would board

every cargo dhow that passed through the region and demand, at gunpoint, a "tariff" in exchange for safe passage. For Ismail, nearly half of the ship's profits would disappear. But short of a gunfight, it was the price he had to pay to do business in the region.

This time, though, the situation was significantly different. The pirates had no idea the dhow was accompanied by a US Navy destroyer. We radioed the *Fletcher*, which was trailing a few miles behind. It wasn't long before she steamed through the flotilla at full speed, directly between us and the bandits. The Iranian "tariff" boats disappeared just as quickly as they'd showed up.

The captain was dumbfounded.

"Sir," he said as we watched the bandit ships disappear over the horizon, "I am forever in your debt."

Our relationship wasn't quite that one-sided, though. As we neared Abu Dhabi, there was a fair bit of confusion coordinating our efforts with the United Arab Emirates Coast Guard. To complicate matters, the UAE Coast Guard officials spoke an Arabic dialect that nobody understood—except for my friend Ismail, that is.

Not only that, but it turned out that the official on the radio was apparently his 'cousin.' So he grabbed the radio and clarified the situation on behalf of our entire flotilla, making our arrival to port much easier than it otherwise would have been.

A few hours later, the dhow was safely in port and we were ready to return to the *Fletcher*. On the deck, Mike and Tommy were laughing and smiling, exchanging handshakes with the crew. Over the past three days they'd all become quite friendly, despite the world of differences between them.

Ismail and I looked on from the bridge.

"Thank you," I said to him, shaking his hand and clapping him warmly on the back.

"No, Captain," he said to me, a smile spreading over his weathered face. "Thank *you*."

I never saw Ismail again. But I like to think he's still out there somewhere on the seas, doing his best to take care of his crew and his family, and maybe even recalling *The Nutty Professor* from time to time.

~~~~~

The beauty of relationships is that they're not always predictable. Of course there are those lightbulb moments where we feel an immediate connection with a person, and know we've just made a lifelong friend. Other times, though—as my experience on the dhow taught me—the connections are more serendipitous. But that doesn't make them any less fulfilling. In fact, it's the times when life throws someone in your path unexpectedly that often lead to the most enriching ends.

And sometimes, they might even keep you out of an Egyptian jail, as I had learned back in the summer of 2005 when I was assigned to VFA-94, a Navy F/A-18 squadron on board the USS *Nimitz* aircraft carrier involved in combat operations over Iraq.

I was one of sixteen pilots and the department head in charge of operations for the squadron. We were at the tail end of our deployment after almost six months in the Persian Gulf, when I was assigned to a pop-up mission to lead a group of five jets to Egypt, where we would participate in an international training event called Exercise Bright Star, led by American and Egyptian forces. It wasn't long before the F/A-18s were catapulted off the deck of the *Nimitz* in succession, with three Navy and two Marine pilots in their cockpits.

It was my first time flying over Egypt, an experience that will stay with me forever. We brought the jets in low on our approach to Beni Suef Air Base, flying directly over numerous pyramids along the way. Sitting in the cockpit of one of the world's most powerful aircraft, the world dropping away below and the desert disappearing forever ahead, I knew I had the greatest job in the world. I was brimming with excitement at the opportunity to visit the historic region I had only previously seen on TV or read about as a kid in *National Geographic*.

Bright Star was a multilateral international exercise. For pilots, it included a variety of training flights, dogfights, and simulated missions. All told, there were more than a dozen countries represented, and the skies were buzzing with aircraft at all hours of the day and night.

One of my first missions was a dogfight with an Egyptian colonel, with me in an F/A-18 and him in an F-16. He was the commanding officer of their country's top-gun school, where their best combat pilots were trained. We fought in clear skies over vast brown deserts cut only by the fertile green strip of the meandering Nile River. He turned out to be a great pilot, so I didn't have much time for sightseeing.

After we finished, we went to his office to debrief the mission. Unlike any debrief I'd ever had, though, this one was accompanied by a steaming pot of tea and a tray of delicious cakes. The colonel, clearly proud of himself at having held his own in a dogfight against an American pilot in an F/A-18, saw this as an opportunity to talk about more than just flying.

The debrief quickly faded into the past as our conversation turned more personal. We discussed our families, our lives back home, our careers. When I told him I had also flown combat helicopters, his mind was blown. From that moment on, he referred to me by my call sign "Chopper" every chance he got, his trademark Egyptian accent curling the word into something far more exotic than it otherwise was. In all honesty, it got to be a little annoying, but I knew the colonel meant well. He was a good man, and simply excited to be spending time with someone he saw as coming from a different world.

Over the next two weeks, the colonel insisted that we train against one another each time we took off. And every time, our debriefs were accompanied with yet another pot of tea, tray of cakes, and more conversation. Eventually it felt like I had found a long-lost kid brother and I grew accustomed to his constant calls of "Chopper! Chopper!"

Exercise Bright Star was set to culminate in a series of joint missions. For fighter pilots, that meant a flyover of more than sixty jets representing every country in the exercise. After takeoff, the jets would rendezvous at a designated location, fly together in formations, then break off into several distinct diamond patterns and fly over the pyramids.

It was a complicated mission to plan. The planes were all taking off from different locations and communicating in different frequencies, usually in very broken English. There was significant room for error, and with that many planes in the sky at once, the consequences could be grave. We also had to stay in perfect formation while we flew over the pyramids, so helicopters could take a series of pictures to document the event.

As frivolous as it may sound, an inordinate amount of energy goes into planning these photo-opportunity operations. Because when the training exercise has been reduced to a mere memory, it's those photographs hanging on the walls of the Pentagon and the Egyptian presidential palace that will remind participating nations of the relationships they solidified along the way. People might forget the dogfights we engaged in, the expertise we developed, and the tactics we refined during those days, but the image of five dozen fighter jets soaring over the pyramids will stand the test of time.

On the morning of the mission, I was walking toward the briefing room in the Egyptian top-gun school when I was stopped by a familiar sound.

"Chopper!" the colonel called. "Come with me."

We walked to his office, where he reflexively served tea and cakes. This time, though, I was a bit preoccupied. With the meeting starting shortly, I felt the need to bring us back to the matter at hand.

"This is a complex mission," I said. "Are you ready to brief this?"

He looked at me slyly. "Chopper my friend," he said, "I am giving *you* the honor *of* briefing this."

"But the brief is in ten minutes," I said.

"I know; you have plenty of time!"

And that was that. To this day I don't know why he wanted me to do it. It could be that he was intimidated by the idea of planning an international operation with dozens of fighter jets in a relatively small piece of sky. On the other hand, it could be that he thought he was paying me the greatest distinction he could imagine. Either way, the responsibility fell on my shoulders. I was taken aback at first, almost annoyed. But as I looked at his smiling face across the desk, I knew there was no malice in his decision. The colonel and I were friends, and I would do what I could.

The briefing room looked like something out of *Star Wars*: dozens of pilots sat there waiting, each in a different-colored uniform or flight suit bearing the flag of their home country. The colonel and I took our places at the front of the room. Then he turned to me and said, "Over to you, Chopper."

Given the circumstances, I did what any sane person would have done in that situation. I told the pilots we were going to take a thirty-minute break. Then I grabbed one of my trusted lieutenants, who had accompanied me from the *Nimitz*, and we hacked out the brief in what little time we had.

To everyone's credit, we pulled off the massive group flight without anyone crashing into a pyramid and causing an international incident. I even managed a quick peek out of the cockpit as I led an international cohort of four jets over the Sphinx and Great Pyramids of Giza.

Two days later we were ready to return to the *Nimitz*. All our maintenance Sailors and equipment had been loaded onto the C-130 Hercules transport aircraft, and the only thing we carried as we walked across the runway toward our waiting jets was a case containing our crypto gear, confidential equipment that enables us to communicate with other US forces while we fly. Crypto gear is exceptionally sensitive material, and it had been kept under lock and key during our entire stay in Egypt. Once we loaded up the jets' radios, the crypto gear would be taken to the waiting C-130.

Out of nowhere, an Egyptian security team pulled up and

surrounded us on the runway. The lead officer, a tall, heavyset Arab with a large mustache, gave me a sinister look. "We need to bring these boxes back to our headquarters," he barked, pointing toward the steel boxes that contained the crypto. I was caught completely off guard by his demand, but that didn't make it any more acceptable.

"I'm sorry, sir," I answered, trying to be as diplomatic as possible under the circumstances. "This is confidential US material and under our custody. We have an agreement with the Egyptian government that we don't have to relinquish it to anybody, including you."

The chief bristled, and accused me of stealing Egyptian intel. No matter how much I tried to convince him otherwise, he refused to back down.

"You're not taking off from this base with those boxes," he snarled.

"I'm not giving them up," I replied.

With no common ground between us, the situation was becoming tense. I could tell the officer was hell-bent on getting the boxes from us, but there was no way short of violence that I was giving them up. The prospect of spending time in an Egyptian prison—not a thought I relished—suddenly seemed very real.

Then I remembered my new friend.

I asked the officer to call the colonel, explaining that he had been our host over the course of the previous two weeks. Luckily, he made the call. Not more than two minutes later, the colonel sped onto the runway in his military vehicle, wheels screeching to a halt within inches of the security officer. He was irate.

I couldn't understand a word the colonel said, but it was obvious he was chewing the rear out of the senior security officer. When the tirade was over, the security officer apologized uncomfortably and slunk off. The colonel walked over to where we stood and held out his hand to me. I knew what was coming.

"Chopper!" he said, smiling broadly as he shook my hand. "Have a safe trip home."

As we flew over the pyramids one last time on our way back to the *Nimitz*, I realized the only thing that got us out of the situation was my relationship with the colonel. In sharing all those pots of tea and trays of cakes, we had become friends. And that friendship proved to be the most formidable weapon I could have brandished during our encounter with security forces on the runway.

I think we're better people when we open our hearts and minds to others. Whether it's a neighbor, a stranger on the street, or perhaps even a mildly annoying colonel who seems infatuated with your call sign, relationships can be unexpected gifts, but ones that can change our lives in profound ways.

~~~~~

In 2010, I was sent to live in Europe to serve as a US staff officer in a NATO command in charge of military operations in the Mediterranean. My family and I were stationed in Naples, Italy, a bewilderingly paradoxical city that's at once incredibly beautiful yet also gritty. "A pretty lady with dirty feet," is how it was once described.

At one moment you'd swear the crazy Neapolitans would like nothing better than to run you over as they career their vehicles through the city at breakneck speeds. At the same time, they are the most loving, family-oriented people I've ever met, and will bend over backward to demonstrate their innate hospitality at every opportunity. On more than one occasion, Mary, the boys, and I were wandering the streets of downtown Naples, only to have random grandmothers and grandfathers stop us outside their homes with gifts of free food as we walked by. When they flatly refused my offers to pay for their hospitality, I realized all they wanted in return for their generosity was our obvious appreciation for their culinary skills—which they had in abundance.

Professionally, my days in Naples were almost exclusively spent in an office. It was not a welcome situation for a Navy fighter pilot, but I was no stranger to long hours at a desk and knew I could get the job done.

It's very easy for Americans to wear our work ethic as a badge of honor. We work hard, and we work a lot. To the contrary, Europeans seem to float through life, gracefully balancing their considerable work responsibilities with the other parts of their lives.

For one thing, Europeans are very good about taking vacation every year. Most people in Europe get at least a month of "holiday" every year, and they are passionate about utilizing it. We witnessed that fact often during our two years in Naples. No matter what was going on in the rest of the world, the Italians made a point of taking time off, usually in August, when most businesses other than those in the service industry shut down.

Those of us in the US military also earn a substantial amount of vacation—two and a half days of vacation for every month worked, or thirty days a year. And yet, I've known very few people who have been able to actually take advantage of those days on a regular, yearly basis, let alone at one time. In fact, if someone did manage to take all thirty days in a single year, I guarantee the prevailing sentiment among their peers would be that they're a slacker.

The motivation to work is so strong that I know of situations where what we call "flag officers"—very senior officers such as admirals or generals—have been stricken with life-threatening events such as heart attacks and still needed to be ordered by *their* superiors to take time off. This ten-day "vacation" is actually mandated by the military for senior officers, and the officers in question are even prohibited from taking their phones with them, to prevent them from working. Yet despite all that, I have still had admirals tell me to call them if anything came up in their absence.

This was my personal bias as I walked into work that first day. The NATO office was housed in an old orphanage, a rambling mansion that had once served as Mussolini's headquarters. I was part of a twelve-nation collaboration called Strike Force NATO, whose goal was to coordinate military operations throughout the Mediterranean region. As a piece of the US Navy's contribution to the operation, I was in charge of coordinating maritime NATO air operations in the Mediterranean and Baltic Seas, and responsible for ensuring the security of the Mediterranean Sea. This included continually patrolling its waters for refugees and migrants, countering the piracy that was prevalent in that part of the world at the time, performing search-and-rescue operations, and training our pilots so they'd be ready in the event that a conflict ever took place.

Like any professional staff, the 120 of us in the office all needed to work together to be effective. Only this time we were challenged by the fact that we came from a dozen different countries, each with its own culture and language. To make matters worse, I was often frustrated in those early days by my colleagues, many of whom did not seem to share my sense of urgency for what I believed at the time to be "critical" PowerPoint briefs and constant instruction rewrites (but clearly weren't!).

I love coffee as much as the next guy, but the Italians—well, they *really* love their coffee. So much so, in fact, that every day at around 9:00 a.m. and again at 11:00 a.m. (and often again at 2:00 p.m.), they would stop whatever they were doing to venture out to a local café for an espresso. In their classic Italian way, they always invited everyone in the office to join.

Initially I was resistant to the idea. Very resistant, in fact. I was eager to make an impression in this international environment, so I gave 110 percent to my work, all the time. There was always a task to do that was far more important than something as trivial as coffee. In my mind, it was the Americans who were doing the lion's share of the work, while the Europeans were always disappearing for their darn coffee breaks.

Then I met Luigi Fazio.

Luigi was a lieutenant colonel in the Italian military, a portly, fiftyish-year-old fellow with dark eyes set in a round face that radiated kindness. Every morning, Luigi would invite me for coffee. And every morning, I refused. Finally, one day, Luigi spoke up.

"Chopper," he said in his imperfect English, "you Americans think if you work hard that we're going to trust you. But what you really need to do is spend time with us *outside* of work, so we can get to know you. Then we can trust you. That's the essence of trust."

I considered Luigi's comments and realized he might be right. Here we had been working elbow to elbow for months, but I knew virtually nothing about the people I was sharing space with, other than their professional duties and responsibilities. So I went for coffee with Luigi and the others. We went at 9:00. We went again at 11:00. And more often than not, we even went at 2:00. Soon that foray to the café became a daily ritual, a welcome break to step outside the realm of work and into the lives of my new friends.

Each break lasted only ten or fifteen minutes. (Italians don't sit for coffee like many others do. They order an espresso at the bar, stand there for a few minutes drinking and chatting, then head on their way.) But over time, those minutes grew into something much more. At some point along the way, we crossed over from coworkers to friends.

Eight months after I joined the staff, NATO was called into a different type of action when Muammar Gaddafi, the de facto leader of Libya, mobilized his forces against his own people after they had organized a series of antigovernment rallies in Benghazi, a city in the northern part of the country. As the protests intensified (the demonstrators eventually took control of Benghazi, and began protesting in Tripoli), Gaddafi began using lethal force against them.

In surprisingly swift fashion, the UN Security Council condemned Gaddafi's actions and authorized military action against Gaddafi, a joint NATO mission called Operation Unified Protector.

The military action began with a separate American operation called Operation Odyssey Dawn, during which I was deployed as an air operations strike planner on the USS *Mount Whitney*, our command ship in the Mediterranean. When this part was finished and Operation Unified Protector was about to launch, I returned to the NATO office in Naples to help coordinate international efforts there.

It was grueling. As deputy director of targeting, I didn't sleep for more than a couple of hours each night for weeks. Our team's job was to utilize intelligence and surveillance to locate, analyze, and validate military targets across Libya deemed to be facilitating attacks on the country's innocent citizens. In doing so, we had to be exceptionally careful to ensure we could effectively strike the military targets while simultaneously ensuring no collateral damage occurred.

The stakes were high, the stress level intense. But in those moments, when we were at the tail end of an eighteen-hour day and there was still a seemingly insurmountable amount of work to get done and lives on the line, the Europeans—those people I had once considered lazy slackers always dashing off for an espresso—were right there beside me, working day and night. They refused to go home until I did and were constantly trying to figure out ways to do things better and smarter. In the end, they were never afraid of hard work when it was necessary.

And through it all, we continued our espresso breaks. Because as Luigi will tell you to this day, it was the friendships we had forged and the culture of camaraderie we had built that actually enabled us to work better together. So not only did we become friends, but we also became better professionals along the way.

Operation Unified Protector would go on to became one of the most successful international air campaigns ever undertaken. After thousands of laser- and GPS-guided air strikes, we crippled Gaddafi's forces and saved the lives of untold thousands of Libyans, all with minimal damage to civilian infrastructure. Yet when the campaign was over, there were no high-fives and no celebrations. Together our international group of disparate professionals breathed a collective sigh of relief, comforted in the knowledge that by coming together and staying in step we had done the best job we possibly could. (I was subsequently awarded two Defense Meritorious Service Medals by the Navy for my role in the operation.)

As that experience taught me, the team can be stronger when the connections between its individual parts are stronger. It is a lesson I tried to share with those around me as well, particularly as I rose in rank. When I addressed my squadron or crew, I often made sure to reiterate Luigi's point.

"Your true impact in this world," I'd say, "is not solely defined by your own capabilities, but by the relationships you have with other people. They will either magnify your capabilities or you will magnify theirs. But collectively, it will make us a much stronger team."

And while I can't always manage to convince my colleagues to head out for one, two, or perhaps even three coffee breaks a day, I've carried Luigi's lesson—as well as those from Egypt and the Persian Gulf—with me ever since. Life is about relationships.

Whether it's your partner or spouse, a lifelong friend, or the person you pass in the supermarket, it's important to remember that we're all people just trying to get by, take care of ourselves, and look after our families. We might have different visions, come from different cultures, and be products of vastly different upbringings, but in the end our similarities far outweigh our differences. And by opening our hearts and minds to the possibility of friendship—no matter how alien and far-fetched it may seem in the moment—we begin to see the good in the world, make ourselves better people, and enjoy the ride a bit more.

As for Luigi Fazio, well, I tried to honor the things he taught me by going out and buying an expensive Italian espresso machine. The coffee doesn't taste quite the same as it did in Naples, but the memories are pretty sweet.

Chapter 2

Learn Like You're Going to Live Forever

Truth be told, as a kid I would have skipped college and gone straight to flight school, if I'd been allowed to. My father was an Air Force veteran, so I spent my early childhood living on Nellis Air Force Base in Las Vegas, surrounded by airplanes and fighter jets. For a young boy, those aircraft represented everything I wanted from life: adventure, power, travel, excitement. I went as far as saving my allowance at the ripe old age of six to buy an encyclopedia of fighter aircraft from the local bookstore, which I have kept to this day. I might be dating myself, but the movie *Top Gun*—which came out while I was in high school, after we had moved to Santa Rosa, California—put into words and images what I had been dreaming for my whole life to that point. So when I entered the United States Naval Academy in Annapolis, Maryland, I had one goal in mind: get into flight school and become a pilot.

While I did make it into flight school, fighter jets were not in my immediate future. I was a strong student, but when I finished flight school, the needs of the Navy at the time dictated that there were only a handful of jet slots to be had, and those went to the men and women at the very top of the class. At first it was frustrating, but I got my next-best choice and was chosen for advanced helicopter pilot training. That said, I never let go of my enthusiasm for jets.

Being a helicopter pilot was cool in its own right, especially during the early days of my career with the Easyriders in Barbers Point, Hawaii. Flying a combat chopper is a complicated undertaking, but once you master the machine, it's like driving the world's coolest pickup truck, with a buddy right beside you and a rescue swimmer in the back. You can take a chopper almost anywhere and do amazing things with it.

On some missions we'd search for submarines, then track them from above. We'd carry parts and cargo between naval vessels, ferry patients during medical emergencies, and on Sundays we'd become the "Holy Helo" and transport a chaplain to other Navy ships in the area to conduct religious services.

The spectacular scenery only added to the experience. Below us, the five primary volcanoes of the islands rose to their blackened, jagged peaks, only to fall away again to lush green forests, sheer ocean cliffs, and misty plateaus, all rimmed by pristine tropical beaches and turquoise waters.

On most of our training flights—or *hops*, as we call them—we would make sure to fly the choppers over the island's best surfing beaches before heading back to base. After landing and debriefing, we'd head to the maintenance board, where we'd share a vital military secret with our peers: which beach had the best surfing conditions that day. It got to the point where the first thing everyone did when they arrived at work was check out the maintenance board to plan their surfing sessions later that day.

After about seven years as a chopper pilot and five moves around the country, I had become a full lieutenant. The money was good, my career was fulfilling, and I was very happily married, with two children at home. But when I heard that the Navy's Aviation Transition Board was about to accept applications for pilots who wanted to switch "communities" and learn to fly other aircraft, I felt I owed it to myself to at least consider the possibility of moving to fighter jets.

It wouldn't have been a problem to turn the opportunity aside. I loved being a helicopter pilot and could have easily settled into that life for my entire career. All in all, I was content and comfortable.

On top of that, making the transition from helicopters to jets would mean two more years of education and training, at least two more moves for my young family, and a whole bunch of unknowns for me. Nevertheless, the desire to grow, to learn, and to improve was strong. So I did what any red-blooded American would do in that situation: I asked my wife.

Mary was all for the idea, if only because she knew how badly I had always wanted to fly jets. So I submitted my name for consideration, knowing that only a few select individuals were chosen for the program each year. This time, I was one of them.

We first moved to the naval air station in Kingsville, Texas, where I began training on the McDonnell Douglas T-45 Goshawk single-engine jet. It was a challenging time: not only did I have to retrain from helicopters to jets, but I also had to grow comfortable with the fact that I was usually the most senior guy in the room, which in that situation was not necessarily a blessing.

I learned pretty quickly that I couldn't let my ego get in the way of my education. The way I saw it, if I was worried about making a mistake in front of junior officers, I should never have agreed to jet training. So I focused on the task at hand and dedicated myself to becoming the best damn fighter pilot I could be.

When I was a student in flight school the first time around, after graduating from Annapolis, those of us who weren't flying on a particular day spent most of our time on the beach, with maybe an hour or two of studying thrown in for good measure. This time, however, my focus was on mastering every aspect of jet training. So if I wasn't in the air, I was studying and preparing. Every week, I committed 40–60 hours to the task, irrespective of the flight schedule. I never wanted to be unprepared when I sat in the cockpit and wanted to show everyone in the class that even though I came with a host of real-world flying experience, I would never put my feet up and rest on my laurels.

After a year in Kingsville, we moved to the Navy's air station in Lemoore, California, where the training would escalate to the major leagues of fighter jets, the McDonnell Douglas/Boeing F/A-18 Hornet.

The F/A-18 is a beast of a machine, and everything a would-be pilot dreams of flying. Boasting twin turbo jet engines, the Hornet can reach speeds of almost 1,200 mph (Mach 1.8) at an altitude of nearly 50,000 feet. Throw in laser-guided and GPS bombing capabilities and a 20mm nose-mounted rotary cannon that can shred enemy craft in a matter of seconds, and it's easy to see why it represented the pinnacle of the flying experience for combat pilots (the F/A-18 has since been surpassed in capabilities by the most advanced fighter jet ever created, the Lockheed Martin F-35 Lightning II).

I will never forget the first time I piloted an F/A-18. As I climbed into the cockpit for the first time, my excitement was palpable—not only to me, but to my instructor pilot Smokey, who sat in the aft cockpit ejection seat behind me. And while this was old hat for her, I was noticeably nervous as I eased the jet onto the runway.

"Nothing to worry about, Chopper," she said calmly to me through my headset. "Just like you've practiced dozens of times in the simulator."

After eleven months, our training in Lemoore culminated with the most thrilling and challenging exercise for any Navy fighter pilot: landing an F/A-18 on the deck of an aircraft carrier. Some have called it the definitive skill that sets naval aviators apart from all other pilots. The difference, of course, is the runway.

On land, a fighter pilot can have as much as 12,000 feet to land. On a carrier, you've got all of 300 feet, so it's an exercise that demands every ounce of focus and preparation. The challenge is complicated by the fact that an aircraft carrier is a moving target, often heaving and swaying on the swells of the ocean. On final approach, the pilot makes countless tiny adjustments to line the jet up perfectly with the ship. Even then, the F/A-18 typically hits the deck at over 150 mph. There's little room for error.

Yet as challenging as a daytime landing may be on an aircraft carrier, it pales in comparison to doing it at night. The ship floats in the middle of open water; from altitude it seems like little more than a dimly lit postage stamp on a vast black background. There's no horizon, no point of reference. It's a frightening undertaking for even the most experienced pilot. But for a rookie fighter pilot doing it for the first time, it can be paralyzing.

It's not like we get to this point unprepared, either. The first time a fighter pilot lands on an aircraft carrier at night, he or she has already landed the jet on an airstrip in similar conditions at least one hundred times, not to mention countless deck night landings in the simulator. We are trained to be unflinching, almost robotic in our actions as we approach the deck, obsessively scanning the plane's HUD (head-up display) for the three things that have been drilled into our heads since day one of flight school: meatball, lineup, angle of attack.

Meatball refers to the glideslope (or "lens"), a vertical guidance system mounted on the left side of the ship that indicates the plane's deviation from its optimal path of descent and tells the pilot whether he or she is coming in too high or too low. We call it a "meatball" or "ball," because of the shape of the light when viewed from the cockpit. Lineup means the jet is headed directly toward the white centerline on the deck of the carrier, while angle of attack means you're flying the jet in the correct profile and at the right speed. In the final few seconds before hitting the deck, the pilot's eyes reflexively follow a neurotic triangular pattern across these three visual targets: meatball, lineup, angle of attack; meatball, lineup, angle of attack. We repeat it over and over again in our heads, until we've landed safely.

Every once in a while, though, you can't help but peer out through the darkness and actually contemplate the fact that you're about to land a fifty-thousand-pound piece of machinery traveling at 150 mph on the world's smallest runway. Those are the "Oh my God" moments for aircraft carrier pilots, when we feel like we've been asked to step into the tee box of a par 3 and hit a hole in one. With hundreds of people watching. In the dark. It feels impossible, but such thoughts evaporate the instant you realize your scan pattern has been interrupted and precious seconds of concentration and preparation have been lost.

In the meantime, tucked away somewhere in the back of your mind are the videos and images you've seen throughout your training of landings that went wrong, jets hitting the back of a ship in a ball of fire and skidding across the flight deck. So we don't have to be too imaginative to understand the consequences of human error.

In those instances, all a pilot can do is remind himself or herself that we've done this before. Stick to the procedures and everything will be okay. Meatball, lineup, angle of attack. In the best-case scenario, the plane's five-foot tailhook is able to grab and "trap" one of the four arresting cables on the flight deck. In some cases the pilot flies too high, the tailhook misses all the arresting cables, and you have to go to full power on the throttles, circle back around, and do it all over again. We call this a "bolter."

During our training in Lemoore, student pilots would fly out to an aircraft carrier somewhere off the coast, where we were then graded according to how well we landed over the course of ten daytime traps (deck landings) and six nighttime traps: how smooth we were, which wire we caught, how well we stayed on the glideslope, which is the angle at which the jet approaches the flight deck (3.5 degrees is optimal). An important part of this assessment was what we call the boarding rate, the percentage of flights successfully landed without bolters.

For an experienced pilot, a typical boarding rate is usually around 99 percent. When you're training, it's between 80 and 90 percent. Mine was on the lower end of that scale, so when I walked in for my final assessment before graduating from the program, I wasn't feeling exceptionally confident, despite the fact that I was a lieutenant commander select, and at least four years senior to Lieutenant Ash (call sign Kiss), who would give me my final assessment.

"Chopper," he said, "the minimum requirements to graduate are a boarding rate above eighty percent and overall grades over 2.80. Your grades are 2.85 and your boarding rate is eighty percent. So technically, you could graduate and move on."

Ash had found himself in a very difficult situation. Here he was, grading a senior officer who hadn't really performed at a level to see him confidently graduate from the program.

"I want to have a conversation with you," he continued, "because you've been in the fleet before as a helicopter pilot and you're more senior than most. So if you feel comfortable with your skills, I'm going to recommend you qualify and move on to the fleet. But I'd like to know what you're thinking. Because you didn't do as well as you could have, and there are still some areas that you need to work on."

His words did not come as a shock to me. I knew my boarding rate was far from perfect, and I also needed to improve my ability to smoothly control the jet's vertical descent rate and my tendency to be overpowered on landing, both of which increased the likelihood that I would bolter. What made it even harder to swallow was that to that point in my career, I had never received what we call a signal of difficulty (SOD). This would be the first hiccup in my flight training, ever. Add to that the fact that only about 20 percent of training pilots didn't finish the program on their first attempt, and you can see how tempting it was to use my rank and seniority to push me through the program.

In the end, though, I knew I couldn't. Physics is unforgiving, and if you screw up in a jet, it doesn't care what your rank is. So professionally, you have to be as good as you can be. Personally, my goal was not to be just good enough. And if that meant going back for more training, then I would have to shelve my ego and open my mind to learning even more.

"Kiss," I said, "what would you say if I was a brand-new student? Because I think you're going to tell me that you would recommend I go back and I do it again."

"That's exactly what I'd do," he answered.

The decision was made. I knew it wasn't a punitive thing and that Kiss was only trying to help me fine-tune my capabilities, so I agreed to the extra training. I was enrolled in another four-week class with a completely new set of pilots and did the whole thing all over again, from the simulator to landing on the carrier.

Was I disappointed initially? Absolutely. The other men and women in my initial class—all of whom were my juniors in rank— all qualified and were assigned to their first squadrons in the fleet. But at the same time I realized that I was being given a chance to continue to refine my skills. And even though much of the training was going to be basic and repetitive, I refused to waste the opportunity. The way I saw it, this was another opportunity to focus on the most critical part of the job, and you can't have a career as a Navy fighter pilot without being able to do it safely. A month later, my landing grades and boarding rate were through the roof.

In the end, the experience taught me as much about life and learning as it did about flying. It's okay to fail and to be less than perfect, as long as you don't give up and you continue to push your own limits. What's more important is that we are honest enough with ourselves to recognize our deficiencies, and be willing to address them. I accepted Kiss's tacit challenge to be the best version of myself, pushed through any discomfort my ego may have caused, and came out better on the other side.

~~~~~

It may not have been *quite* how *Top Gun* had portrayed it, but life as a Navy pilot was as adventurous as I had imagined, perhaps even more so. To begin with, the flying was incredible. From the first day I sat in the cockpit of an F/A-18, to my last flight in February 2022, which saw me and a couple of my closest friends soaring over the Sierra Nevadas, it was never lost on me how incredibly fortunate I was to be entrusted with a $70 million machine. But what I hadn't anticipated was how much I'd fall in love with the lifestyle, despite the amount of time it kept me away from Mary and our family. Whether it was feeling the excitement of an impending combat deployment or the awe that accompanied port-of-call visits to far-flung countries, the months and years to come were punctuated with mind-blowing experiences.

The other thing I hadn't banked on was the feeling of esprit de corps that came with Navy life. One of the best things about being a Navy pilot was that I got to share my experiences with some of my closest friends and colleagues, whether it was with a squadron mate like Casey as my wingman or a group of pilots swapping sea stories in the ready room before a mission. In the end, it was this sense of teamwork and camaraderie that kept me in the Navy for my entire career, because it actually amplified the positive feelings that came along with each experience. I was seeing the world (a lifelong military career means you move *a lot*), spending time with an amazing group of people, and flying some of the most sophisticated machines ever designed.

I had been in the Navy for almost twenty years, was happily married, with three boys, had attained the rank of commander, and had served as the commanding officer of the Mighty Shrikes of VFA-94, an F/A-18 squadron in Lemoore, California. As had been the case when I made the transition from helicopters to jets, it would have been easy to stay on my current path for the rest of my career. But in the back of my mind, a notion had taken seed and was beginning to grow: commanding an aircraft carrier, the pinnacle job for a career naval aviator.

I knew that each year, the Navy selected a few naval aviators to train to become commanding officers of the nation's eleven aircraft carriers. For a Navy officer, it was the Mount Everest of career advancement, and if you complete the job successfully, you have a good chance of being promoted to admiral. But you can't command an aircraft carrier without first graduating from the Navy's nuclear power school.

Why nuclear power school? The US Navy has more nuclear-powered vessels in active service than any other navy on earth. All of our aircraft carriers and submarines are powered by nuclear reactors, which make them incredibly self-sufficient. A nuclear-powered vessel can run on a virtually infinite power source, which makes it far more capable—and complex—than its diesel-powered counterparts.

In the US, nuclear-powered naval propulsion was the brain-child of then captain Hyman G. Rickover, who began studying its possibilities in the late 1940s. Less than a decade later Rick-over's dream became reality and the Navy started incorporating nuclear reactors into its submarines. Aircraft carriers followed shortly thereafter.

As you'd imagine, nuclear propulsion is extremely com-plex. That's why it's essential for the commanding officers of these ships to understand the process as thoroughly as possible. Nuclear training allows the Navy's commanding officers to make informed decisions based on their intimate knowledge of science and engineering, not just the opinions of others on board.

For most sane people, the thought of going back to school after having spent twenty years in a career is a hard no. Nuclear power school is an intense two-year training program of master's level courses in science, math, and nuclear engineering. By the time you're done, you know how a reactor plant is made, and the chemistry, pressure, and temperature of every drop of water in the system; can trace the path of an electron from a bus-sized generator to a lightbulb five hundred feet away; have memorized every element in the periodic table; and can calculate everything from advanced differential equations to radioactive reactions at the subatomic level. Daunting? Yes. But it's the only way to become commanding officer of an aircraft carrier.

I wasn't sure I could make it through the course. I was an average student at best in college, and that had been two decades earlier. At the same time, I knew it was a chance to challenge myself, advance my career, and learn something new. That said, I first had to discuss the possibility of yet another move with Mary.

As rewarding as a military career might be, its itinerant lifestyle (we would change addresses twenty times in thirty years) can take a toll on a family. For Mary, it meant that she had to dampen her career aspirations and instead provide continuity and stability for the family while I was away, often for months at a time. For the boys, it meant regularly changing schools and making new friends, often during their formative childhood and adolescent years. For me, it meant coming to grips with the fact that I wasn't going to be there for many of life's important events. There have been too many missed birthdays, anniversaries, and Christmases to count.

Luckily for all of us, Mary grew up in a Navy family and had ample experience with constant moves and long deployments. She was the glue that held the family together, and never let the prospect of a new address get in the way of adventure. So with her support, I applied for the program, and was fortunate enough to be accepted. Soon we were on the move again, this time from Naples, Italy, to Charleston, South Carolina.

Most students in the Navy's nuclear power school are junior officers fresh out of college with engineering degrees. They attend the program almost immediately after joining the Navy, and are then assigned to work on submarines or aircraft carriers in the fleet. Only a handful of senior officers attend every year, all destined to command aircraft carriers . . . if they can make it through the course.

Being the senior officer in the room is typically not a disadvantage. But when it comes to advanced education in nuclear engineering, you haven't been in a classroom in two decades, and the rest of your classmates are at the top of their game . . . there's plenty of room to start doubting your decision.

On the day before classes began, I went supply shopping with another commander, a man with the rather unique call sign of Jenny (last name: Craig) and the only other senior officer in the class with me. Among the many items on our list was an engineering calculator. Well, we painfully realized how challenging the next two years were going to be as we gawked at the various makes and models spread out before us. These things *looked like* calculators, but they bore little resemblance to the ones we had used in college two decades before. Eventually we grabbed a couple, hoping they were the right ones.

The next morning, the twentysomethings in the class—a group of bright-eyed and scary-smart young men and women—were coolly comfortable as they set to work on the first problem of the day. It was a very different story for me as I fumbled with the calculator in my hands. I couldn't even figure out how to turn the thing on, let alone use it effectively.

"Jenny," I said, shooting him a commiserating look as he stared blankly at his calculator, "we've got a long way to go to catch up to these kids."

"Sure do, Chopper," he said with a grimace. "Sure do."

That's when the reality of what I had signed up for slapped me in the face. Although my Navy training and subsequent career had often pushed me to my physical and mental limits, these next two years were going to be among the most difficult. I was an accomplished pilot and former commanding officer of a Navy fighter squadron. But mastering the nuances of nuclear physics represented a level of complexity I had yet to encounter in my career.

The first thing I did was accept the challenge and open myself up to the wonderful things I was about to learn. This was an important step, because it was a recognition of the difficulties I would face, and confirmation of my belief in my own abilities to learn new things. I told myself I was going to have to work harder than anyone else in that room, just to be able to keep up. More importantly, I was going to have to recognize just how little I knew, get over any embarrassment I might have, and ask questions every time I didn't understand something. That happened often. Very often.

As I suspected, the schedule was arduous. From Monday to Friday, I left the house early each morning and didn't return until around eight o'clock that night. On one day each weekend I'd spend another seven or eight hours at the school catching up.

The first six months in Charleston were spent exclusively in the classroom, followed by six months that incorporated some fieldwork on the submarine trainer stationed at the base. After Charleston our family had to move yet again, this time to San Diego while I went on to Washington, DC, where I continued my training at the Naval Reactors headquarters, studying the formidable reactors powering the Navy's aircraft carriers.

Finally, after almost two years of study and hands-on training, I was named the executive officer (XO) of my first aircraft carrier, the USS *Ronald Reagan*. As the ship's second in command, my job was to run the floating city of five thousand men and women. Whereas the CO of a ship is more like its mayor, and bears the responsibility of maintaining the ship's culture and ensuring the success of its strategic operations, the XO is its city manager. And while my training and experience to that point had given me insights into helicopters, fighter jets, and nuclear reactors, only hands-on training would teach me the finer points of the *Reagan*'s day-to-day operations, including such glamorous pursuits as sewage, water treatment, supply logistics, church services, barbershops, emergency training, and general upkeep.

I approached my job as a daily exercise in learning something new, not only because I wanted to do the best job I could for the sake of everyone on board, but because I also knew that my success (or failure) as an XO would ultimately dictate whether I'd be promoted to CO of an aircraft carrier or not. The days (and nights) were incredibly long, every minute full of new challenges and responsibilities. At the end of every one I would put my feet up, take a deep breath, and contemplate how much I had learned . . . and still had to learn.

But the hard work and positive attitude paid off. Two and a half years later, I departed the *Reagan* and began ten more months of training to prepare to be the commanding officer of my first ship, the USS *Blue Ridge*, the lead command and communications ship of the Navy's Seventh Fleet, which was stationed in Japan at the time. At 634 gorgeous feet long and weighing almost 20,000 tons, the *Blue Ridge*—the oldest operational ship in the Navy—is capable of carrying almost 1,200 crew and officers.

For senior officers like me, the *Blue Ridge* is one of only a handful of the Navy's larger vessels, both in crew and size, where future commanding officers of aircraft carriers continue their education into how to drive and lead large ships.

As always, the promotion to CO of the *Blue Ridge* came with significant educational responsibilities. I would have to learn a new propulsion system, how to drive a different class of ship, and how to manage the incredibly complex communications systems on board while simultaneously navigating the incredibly busy and contentious waters of the western Pacific Ocean. Daunting though it was, I threw myself into my newfound responsibilities with vigor. As with the *Reagan*, every day was a learning experience, every challenge a chance to do what I could to empower and care for the crew I was now responsible for.

Toward the end of the eighteen-month tour, I was standing on the bridge of the *Blue Ridge*, watching the sun rise to the east with Japan's iconic Mount Fuji behind me, when I received an official message from my admiral. After two years of nuclear power training, two and a half years as the XO of the *Reagan*, and another year and a half as the CO of the *Blue Ridge*, I had achieved the goal I had set for myself back when I first decided to go back to nuclear power school: I would command a US Navy aircraft carrier.

Even then, this was not a time to rest on my laurels and celebrate my success. To the contrary, my education would continue in earnest. In fact, it would take another twelve months of schooling and training before I would actually take over the carrier: more nuclear power training in Washington, DC; ship-driving training in Newport, Rhode Island; and even refresher flight training in the F/A-18 Super Hornet at Lemoore, California.

Looking back, those years were far from easy. It had taken me almost eight years from the day I decided to apply to nuclear power school. The work had been difficult and the commitment significant. I struggled. I beat my head against the wall. I hadn't spent nearly enough time with my family. I'd asked questions that were so rudimentary they left classmates twenty years my junior shaking their heads in disbelief at my ignorance.

But by the time I had finished, I'd learned something I never thought I would learn. If you're willing to take a risk and operate outside your comfort zone, you're going to learn and grow. My guess is that most people in their mid to late forties with established careers would not be willing to go back to square one and retrain for what essentially amounts to a new career with their existing employer. But the experience taught me that if you're willing to take a risk, you can achieve things you may not have imagined possible. Personally, I was much better off for the experience. As a result, I was proud beyond words when the Navy named me the commanding officer of the USS *Theodore Roosevelt*, one of the most storied, most capable, and most impressive ships on earth.

~~~~~

As a general rule, flying fighter jets is expensive . . . and difficult. An F/A-18 eats up approximately thirty gallons of jet fuel every minute (1,800 gallons/hour). When you include the cost of parts, oil, fuel, and maintenance it generally costs over $10,000 per hour to fly, and that doesn't include the extraordinary cost to operate the aircraft carrier that we often launch from. Given such an investment, we have to make sure every second—and dollar—counts.

The postflight debriefing session ("debrief") is our chance to make sure that money is not wasted, and dissect every aspect of every flight, whether a patrol mission over Iraq or a training hop for junior pilots just out of flight school.

These sessions can be intense. A one-hour training flight can be followed by a three- or four-hour debrief. We watch videos of the flights; we discuss instrumentation and maneuvering. Yet no matter how long or complex the debrief may be, they all have one thing in common: everyone leaves their rank at the door when they walk in.

To some, this is an uncommon phenomenon, because the military *loves* rank. Rank defines the nature of the relationship between parties and sets out a clear and orderly chain of command. From the junior enlisted E-1 Seaman Recruit to an O-10 Fleet Admiral, everybody knows their place in the food chain. The aviation debrief is one of the few times that the hierarchy is ignored. The rationale behind this phenomenon is simple: everyone can learn valuable things from anyone else in the room, no matter how junior they may be. By putting all pilots on equal footing, we all have equal opportunity to learn from one another.

Egalitarian though it may be, the concept is difficult for some pilots to comprehend initially, especially junior officers who have been conditioned to treat their superior officers with deference. That's why as a senior officer I made sure to start each of my debriefs with the same message.

"Folks," I'd say, "let me remind you that we are all here to learn, and that's why there are no ranks in debriefs. For the duration of this session, everyone in this room is equal. Now let's get to work."

To help junior pilots become accustomed to the concept, we'd go so far as to completely remove people's names from the debrief and simply refer to the call sign of the flight and jet in question. The result would be something like, "During the off-target egress, Hobo 52 was supposed to target the hostile group to the North but targeted the South group instead, therefore allowing the North enemy group to launch missiles at friendly fighters." (We don't really shoot missiles at each other in training.)

The goal of these sessions is an open and collegial atmosphere where everybody has the opportunity to share, learn, and grow. As I became a senior officer who was also lucky enough to be an active pilot, it was also a chance for me to model behavior for the junior officers in the room. Junior officers eventually turn into senior officers, and the last thing I wanted to create were senior officers who thought they knew everything.

I continued this in my senior leadership roles throughout my career. My goal in those situations was to show everyone on board how much I believed in the idea that everyone could learn from everyone else, irrespective of rank or position. To help demonstrate this as a captain, I would often show up unannounced at one of the ship's many workshops and simply start asking questions.

"Good morning, buddy," I'd say. "What are you guys up to today?"

The first few times, the result wasn't exactly what I had hoped. Any time the captain walks into a space—any space—on a ship, the Sailors who work there are noticeably nervous. Have the captain then ask what they do, and it's a recipe for instant perspiration.

"You're the expert here," I'd say. "I'm not quizzing you, I just want to learn something about this. Teach me."

Eventually, though, the crew got to know me and my methods, and became comfortable with the notion that I was simply trying to learn a little bit more about them as people, about the ship, and the function their shop or department served.

Most Sailors were extremely proud to show me what they did and explain the role they played in the larger organization of the carrier. Equally important, I believe, was that I showed them how comfortable I was demonstrating my own ignorance.

I did this on more than one occasion. Sometimes I even took it to our larger meetings and briefs, where I made a point of calling people out when they let military jargon get in the way of a clear message.

Like any profession, the military has its own language . . . and loves acronyms. In fact, I'd go so far as to say that if there's a way—any way—to shorten a phrase by slapping a bunch of letters together, the military will find a way. This is fine if you're intimate with that particular system or department. But in a large briefing session that includes Sailors and officers from a floating city of five thousand, these acronyms can get insanely confusing and can sometimes leave important folks out of the conversation as a result:

"It is very important that all DIVOs and CPOs assigned as PLs verify their respective COSAL and APLs ASAP so we don't fall behind on our CU phases and PCD, delay the completion of our PIA, and risk the ETD of our upcoming CQ and COMPTUEX."

Translation: Make sure that you have everything you need on board to finish the ship repairs so we can get under way on time to begin training.

So as a leader interested in setting a positive example and as a human being who believes he can learn from anyone at any time, I made a point of raising my hand every time someone used an acronym that sounded remotely alien.

"Hold on a second," I'd say, raising my hand. "Remind me what *GUI* means?"

The way I saw it, one of three things would happen. First, people might laugh at me because I was the only one in the room who apparently didn't know what a graphical user interface—or touchscreen—was. Second, the others who didn't know what *GUI* meant (but were afraid to ask) now had greater insight into what was happening.

Third and most important, though, was the fact I was setting an example for my shipmates that admitting what you don't know is the first step to learning and growing, as people and as an organization.

Some commanding officers were so anti-acronym that they tried to ban them entirely from debrief sessions. One of my finest mentors, Captain Chris Bolt (call sign Bolter)—who was the captain of the USS *Ronald Reagan* when I was its executive officer—was one such person. Bolter's stand against acronyms was not always relished by the crew (his debriefs took a *long* time), but it created an atmosphere where there was little, if any, room for confusion. More importantly, it was Bolter's subtle way of admitting that even though he was the commanding officer of the ship, he recognized that he didn't know everything.

While I didn't follow directly in Bolter's footsteps, his message was never lost on me. If you're all puffed up on seniority, worried about your pride, and concerned with how you appear, you're going to miss out on one of life's greatest gifts.

Because when you stop learning, you stop growing and you stop improving. I chose to be curious, always trying to keep my mind and heart open to the new and unknown, no matter how difficult the challenge may have been. As a result, I was fortunate to learn how to fly helicopters and fighter jets, command a squadron, operate a nuclear reactor, and become the captain of one of the greatest aircraft carriers ever built.

CHAPTER 3

When in Doubt, Be Kind

There are many rules in life. Only one of them, however, is golden. And while the Golden Rule has been phrased and rephrased a hundred different ways for millennia, the essence of it is always the same: treat other people the way you want to be treated. For me, that default position has hopefully always been one of kindness.

I'll admit it's not always easy. We're human, after all, and the foundation of the human condition is that we're far from perfect. To make matters worse, there are times when people do or say things that make our blood boil and we feel a primal, almost irresistible urge to lash out.

As a California native, my thoughts invariably go to driving. When we're behind the wheel, it's all too easy to get frustrated by the actions of others. Sometimes we perceive those "offenses" as so egregious that it makes us drive more aggressively. Maybe we won't make room for the person who's desperately trying to merge or perhaps we lose control and actually cut someone off as a result of our anger. And what do we gain? Absolutely nothing. Believe me, I've done my share of stupid things behind the wheel and have regretted every single one.

But I have never regretted being kind while driving, even if it seemed to come at my own expense. All it takes is a simple change in perspective. As Mary will often remind me, the person in front of me might be having the worst day of his or her life. They might be rushing to the hospital to see a loved one, or maybe just got fired from the job that's keeping their family afloat.

By doing something as incredibly simple and seemingly meaningless as letting them merge, I may have just made their day—and *my* day—a little better. Random acts of kindness don't have to be headline-making grand gestures. Whether it's on the road, waiting for the next wave when surfing, or just about anytime in life . . . sometimes even the simplest actions can make a big difference.

As a kid growing up among the rolling hills of Santa Rosa, California, my household was dominated by the female energy of my mother and three younger sisters, all four of whom are incredibly strong women, as strong as any fighter pilot. And while I loved the time I spent with my father, mother, and three sisters, working and playing sports were two great ways for me to be on my own or with the groups of "brothers" I didn't have in my household.

I also found time for myself through work. My first job was as a paper boy. Seven days a week, I would wake up early, slip rubber bands or plastic bags over a hundred folded copies of the *Press Democrat*, then ride around our suburban neighborhood on my bike, expertly tossing them on people's porches before school started. On some days it was pouring rain up there in Northern California, and the last thing I wanted to do was deliver those damn papers. If it happened to be a Saturday or Sunday, I'd often call in the cavalry.

"Dad?" I'd ask, peering into my parents' still-dark bedroom, pretending I believed he was actually awake. "Do you think you could drive me to deliver the papers?"

It would have been easy for him to say no. He would have been justified in telling me that delivering papers in a downpour was part of the job I had signed up for. But he didn't. More often than not, my dad would say, "Sure thing, Brett," hop out of bed, and help me.

I knew he didn't have to, but I sure did appreciate it. It was that small act that made me realize how far a little kindness goes. And despite what the naysayers and taskmasters out there might think, my dad's help never caused me to lose sight of my responsibilities. I didn't start asking him for help on sunny days, and often went out in the rain on my own. But his kind gesture made me feel better about myself, about him, and about the world.

Whether it was the product of such acts of kindness or simply my personality, I have always operated on the fundamental belief that most people want to do good in the world. Sometimes that message gets lost in the fog of professional stress, to-do lists, efficiency, and profitability. But individually, I think everybody is trying to do the right thing, work hard, and be a good person, regardless of what they do for a living.

That conviction guided the way I interacted with those around me throughout my Navy career, irrespective of my position or rank at the time. As a leader, I tried to approach every situation with an understanding about other people's inherent desire to do good. It never let me down. Holding on to that fundamental principle—treating people the way I wanted to be treated—helped me be the best leader I could possibly be. I believe it helped those around me be the best they could be as well.

There were many times when I could have let my emotions get the best of me and gone on to criticize or belittle people. But I suspect such behavior would have had the opposite effect of what I was trying to achieve as a leader. Instead of training and teaching them—which ultimately allowed them to learn, grow, improve, and, most importantly, get the job done—such outbursts would only have served to create stressed-out, anxious automatons whose only goal was to avoid me or, worse, appease me.

I've seen it happen many times. I've worked for leaders in fairly senior positions who were, simply put, jerks. As a result, the people who worked for them lived in constant fear of rebuke. Ask these people what they were doing and why they were doing it, and their answers were always the same: "Because the boss wants it this way." Not because it was the right thing to do. Not because they were free to use their own intellect and ingenuity to solve a problem. Simply because the boss wanted it that way.

Tell someone what to do and they'll do the task you set before them. Teach them how to think for themselves and they'll solve problems on their own for the rest of their lives.

At the end of the day, the only person on earth who dictates how you will react in any given situation is *you*. Being a jerk is easy. It takes zero strength of character to shoot someone down, belittle them, or make them feel small. Kindness, understanding, compassion, patience . . . those are the hallmarks of true strength.

~~~~~~~

For decades, the American military has provided its service members with green memorandum books that fit perfectly in the pocket of a uniform or flight suit. Before the advent of smartphones, when electronic note-taking became the preferred method of recording leadership stories, soldiers, Sailors, pilots, and officers would use these books religiously to keep notes and records.

As young officers, we were instructed early in our careers to use our green books to track the leadership lessons we would go on to learn throughout our careers. Doing so, the theory went, would help us identify and distinguish between the good, the bad, and the ugly of leadership styles. Not only would the books end up being reference guides as we advanced, but they would also afford us the opportunity to address the bad stuff we were bound to encounter along the way, sort of green-book therapy for dealing with jerks.

Of the many lessons and examples I recorded in my green books through the years, nobody filled more pages on the positive side of the ledger than Bolter, one of the most influential leaders I ever met. Working as Bolter's executive officer (XO) on the USS *Ronald Reagan* for two years starting in 2014 was a master class in leadership. Yet, interestingly enough, one of the best lessons Bolter ever taught me came after an incident where he let his emotions get the better of him and lost his cool.

During that tour of duty, one of the many tasks Bolter

assigned me as XO was to figure out how to get Wi-Fi on board the *Reagan* when the ship was in port. As it stood, cell coverage was only available on the flight deck, which proved inconvenient for Sailors, especially during poor weather. Bolter wanted the Sailors to have Wi-Fi access on the mess decks where they ate, and for officers and chiefs to have it in the wardrooms and chief's mess. It had never been done before on a large Navy ship. My job was to make it happen.

I ran into roadblocks at every turn. It was cost prohibitive. It would present a security threat to the ship. The pier connections were incompatible. New cables would have to be run on board. Older (aka "salty") leaders thought it would be a distraction. From the internet provider to the technicians at the base to other folks on board the ship, everyone said it couldn't be done. So I took the message back to Bolter: it was time to throw in the towel. He was unimpressed.

"Chopper," he said, "these are all things we can get around. Think about how important it is for our Sailors. And if we're going to take care of our Sailors, this is one way to do it. While we're in port, they want to be able to take a break and eat their meals while they're on their phones. Some of these kids live on the ship and have no other home, so let's make their home as comfortable as possible."

With those marching orders we went out to try again, only to encounter more obstacles. After two more weeks of starts and stops—well after Bolter had hoped to have the Wi-Fi up and running—I went back to him with more bad news, this time with a report in hand and a group of department heads, technicians, and other officers in tow to help explain why it simply couldn't be done.

"Captain," I said as I summed up the report, "I'm afraid it's just not possible. Looks like maybe sometime next year we should be able to do it. But not now."

That's when Bolter's frustrations boiled over.

"Look, XO," he said (he usually called me Chopper). "I didn't say you had the option to throw in the towel. This is important to me because it's important to the Sailors. I feel like you're slow-rolling me, and I'm tired of you guys coming back with reasons why we can't support this. What is not clear about what I expect?"

I was taken aback. To that point, all our interactions had been collegial and friendly, even buddy-buddy. After all, we were the two senior officers on the ship. But this was obviously different.

"All right, sir," I said. "We'll go back and reattack this, and we'll figure it out."

I was extremely frustrated, maybe even angry, because I felt Bolter had singled me out in front of all the other people in the room. I knew I was a good XO and had done all kinds of positive things for the *Reagan* and her crew, and didn't feel like I deserved to be treated like that.

I was still mad by the time I got home. It was very uncharacteristic for me, because I rarely brought the stresses of work into my family life. But this was different. In retrospect, I imagine it was because Bolter had been such an incredibly positive force in my career, which made his words sting that much more.

Then my phone rang. It was Bolter.

"Evening, Captain," I said.

"Hey, Chopper," Bolter said. "I want to apologize for what I said. You're a great XO and you bust your ass every day. The ship is a great ship, and the crew is well taken care of because of how hard you work. I had no right to get that frustrated with you and speak to you that way."

"Thanks, Captain. I really appreciate that."

"That said," he continued, "I want to reiterate that this is really important to me. And I think in the end we'll both see how great it is for the Sailors and will make a huge difference for them. At the same time, I understand your challenges. So let me know how I can help. But I'm sorry for being out of line. You didn't deserve that."

For the second time that day, I was taken aback. Bolter knew me well enough to understand how frustrated I was, and he knew how much there was to be gained by apologizing. He recognized that he had missed an opportunity to guide me and instead had demeaned me. Yet the best part was that he still didn't let me off the hook. He had the strength of conviction to stand by his decision, only this time with a completely different approach.

In an instant, I went from being pissed-off to once again thinking this was the greatest guy I'd ever worked for.

With Bolter's help, we were eventually able to overcome all our obstacles and get Wi-Fi on the ship. And just as the captain had predicted, it made a tremendous difference in our Sailors' lives. We all benefited from not having to go to town, to the base, or up on the flight decks in the pouring rain or scorching sun to use our phones. More than anyone, the Wi-Fi was for that nineteen-year-old kid who had just enlisted, arrived in a floating city of five thousand strangers, and could only connect with his friends and family back home through his phone. The benefits were even more palpable when we eventually deployed to Japan, and now had more than a thousand Sailors living on the ship full-time when we were in port. For those people, having a consistent link to their families was a huge part of their well-being.

The *Reagan* was the first aircraft carrier in the Navy to employ Wi-Fi in port, and set an example that others soon mimicked. In fact, the Navy has actually made this standard practice today, and even figured out how to provide recreational Wi-Fi to Sailors while at sea. I tried to follow in Bolter's footsteps on the ships I commanded thereafter.

For me, the example Bolter set was far more important than the Wi-Fi. He showed that perfection is an elusive goal, and part of being a good leader is recognizing your mistakes and owning them. I also relearned the value of praising in public and reprimanding in private, and how important such a simple mantra could be when it came to the confidence and motivation of the Sailors around me. They became two of the most important lessons in my leadership green book, and I never forgot either one. And as much as I'd like to say that I carried that book with me for the rest of my life, the truth is that I fell in line with the times and soon found myself storing my leadership lessons on my phone. But that never lessened the importance of the messages I wrote down all those years ago.

~~~~~

As Luigi Fazio so eloquently taught me in Italy, working day and night is not necessarily the key to a happy life. And yet the urge to work excessively is very strong with many Americans. In the military, the sentiment of sacrificing everything for your work is even more pervasive. Days off are a sign of weakness. It's all hands on deck, all the time.

In theory, I understand the rationale. After all, a Navy ship is ultimately a warship, and Sailors need to be ready for combat at any moment. At the same time, as commanding officer I never tried to lose sight of the fact that the Sailors in my squadrons and on my ships were not just Sailors, they were people, too: people with family, friends, and loved ones who cared about them.

The brutal reality of military service, however, is that in combat there will be losses. So if an aircraft carrier can't function after suffering casualties, the entire system is flawed. The ship should be combat-ready whether there's five thousand people on board or three thousand people on board. Those left will have to work harder to pick up the slack, but the entire operation should not come to a grinding halt.

That was my mentality when I was the executive officer of the USS *Ronald Reagan*, which was operating off the coast of Japan in the summer of 2016. Being based in Japan meant that all the Sailors assigned to the *Reagan* (and their families) lived at the Navy base in Yokosuka or in the surrounding area. Even though it was a massive base—579 acres strong and housing as many as 25,000 people—the Sailors assigned to the *Reagan* were a small, tight-knit community.

The *Reagan* was in the midst of a series of operations, important training certification exercises in preparation for the upcoming deployment, when it came to my attention that the base's American high school was having its graduation ceremonies soon after we were scheduled to go to sea. Although none of my sons were old enough to have graduated yet (two of them attended school on the Yokosuka base at one point or another), I knew it was an important event for both students and their parents.

The issue came to a head when I received a request chit from a Sailor on board. His only daughter was graduating from high school and he wanted to leave the ship to attend the ceremony with his wife. The chit was written very respectfully and his plan was well considered. Attending the graduation meant the Sailor would be off the ship for a few days. He would have to fly back to the ship as a passenger in a Navy C-2 carrier-based twin-engine plane, but we weren't far from the coast and the C-2 was already going back and forth to the beach every day to pick up parts, supplies, and new Sailors. The Sailor even had one of his shipmates offer to cover for him in his absence.

The chit went through his chain of command, ending with his HOD (head of department). Everyone had denied it.

Except me, that is. I approved the Sailor's request. If the ship couldn't operate with one less Sailor, we had no business being at sea in the first place. It was clear as day to me, but soon the HOD was knocking on my door scratching his head.

"Sir, these are very important training exercises and this Sailor knows we can't approve this request."

I knew he came by his feelings honestly and was concerned about our mission. Before we sailed the *Reagan* from San Diego to Yokosuka, we had swapped crews with another aircraft carrier, which had been operating out of Yokosuka for several years. The *Reagan* was taking the place of this older carrier to become what we call the forward-deployed naval force aircraft carrier of the Seventh Fleet; as a result we inherited half her crew. And while Bolter and I had worked hard to create a positive, supportive, and team-oriented culture on our ship over the previous five years, things had been very different on the ship we relieved.

That carrier had been on high-tempo operations for the last couple of years, and over time its culture had become as rigid as its steel hull. For the thousands of Sailors who were transferred to the *Reagan*, the prevailing philosophy was that the mission trumped everything else: Sailors' wants and needs were secondary. So unless a family member was dying, nobody left. Period.

I welcomed the chance to explain my rationale for approving the request to the HOD; this was a golden opportunity to begin to shape the crew's culture into something our new captain—Buzz, who replaced Bolter—and I wanted. "Why?" I asked. "Why can't we approve this?"

"Well, sir, we need everybody on board when we're under way. What we're doing is important. Our Sailors know that being in the Navy means they're going to miss out on things, even things that may be important."

"Let me ask you something," I replied. "Is the ship going to sink or are we not going to be able to fulfill our mission because of this one Sailor?"

"No, sir," he replied. "But this is a senior Sailor we're talking about."

"I understand that," I answered. "But again, this is a warship and we have to be able to operate even if we lose senior Sailors in combat. I'd like to think that the whole ship won't come to a screeching halt if we lose one person."

"That's true, sir."

"Do you have qualified people to cover for him?" I asked.

"Yes, sir. I do."

"Well, then I think there's no reason to *not* let the Sailor go," I said. "Then he'll get to see his daughter's graduation, which happens only once in a lifetime. Plus, I guarantee you that Sailor's going to come back and work even harder for us because he knows we're going to go out of our way to take care of him."

Despite what I thought was a very sound rationale for my decision, the officer still looked at me quizzically. Clearly I had not addressed all of his concerns, so I asked him what else he had on his mind.

"Sir," he said, "if we do this for one Sailor, then we're certainly going to get more asking for the same thing. The high school has around a hundred kids in each class, so there's a good chance you'll have more than one parent on board this ship with a child graduating. Will they all get to go?"

He paused. "In fact," he added, "my daughter is graduating high school at the same time."

"Well," I asked. "Do you all want to go?"

"I'd venture to guess that at least ten or fifteen of us will want to."

"All right, then, we'll let all of you go," I answered.

He was dumbfounded. Not only was this a radical shift from the culture he had experienced during his previous deployment, but he was struggling to see how the ship would function in the absence of at least a dozen Sailors, including more than a few officers.

"Really?" he asked.

"The same theory applies," I said. "The ship's not going to sink without these people on board."

He pressed on: "But I'm a senior department head. Who's going to cover me?"

"I imagine you've got a deputy, and I assume that deputy is

ready to step in for you because you've been training her or him all along, right?"

"That's correct, sir."

"And as a matter of fact, I bet your deputy would love the opportunity to step up and take over for you."

The officer was beginning to realize that this wasn't a joke after all.

"You're serious?" he asked. "You're gonna let us go?"

"Absolutely," I answered. "But here's the deal: I want you to get the word out and let people know that if they have a child graduating, I'm going to approve them to attend. And we'll fly them back when it's over."

Incredulous, the commander walked off. Then I went to Buzz to get his okay with the plan.

"Chopper," Buzz said smiling, "I agree this is an important event for them. So if you feel good as XO that you can still run the ship without them then, then I'm one hundred percent behind you."

For Buzz and me, it was a golden opportunity to redefine the culture of the ship and show our Sailors that we were going to do everything we could to take care of them. In fact, unlike some ships, where it was "mission above all else," we adopted a new philosophy: *Sailors first, mission always.* The way we saw it, we'd never lost sight of our mission, but we would always make sure our Sailors were taken care of.

Sure enough, I had about a dozen request chits on my desk the next day.

When the graduation was over and the Sailors returned to the *Reagan*, every single one of them sought out Buzz and me to offer their thanks. In fact, many other Sailors and officers—none of whom had anything to do with the graduation—also went out of their way to compliment us on our decision. And while I have no way to quantify an individual Sailor's efforts, I would argue that each one of those people worked harder and was more committed to the ship than ever after they returned.

I carried the philosophy with me when I was named CO of the USS *Theodore Roosevelt*, shortly before Thanksgiving 2019. At that time, the *TR* was performing training work-ups that kept us away from our home base in San Diego for up to six weeks at a time. During those missions, we fine-tuned every aspect of our operations, from firefighting to missile systems, air attacks to navigation, all while being constantly engaged in simulated combat maneuvers both in the air and at sea. At the same time, we were being observed and evaluated by the admiral and his staff, whose job it was to ensure that the ship and her crew were ready to deploy. It was intense and stressful, and demanded 100 percent effort and focus from everyone on board.

The exercises were timed so that the *TR* was scheduled to be at sea from mid-November until just a few days before Christmas, which meant we would all miss Thanksgiving at home with our friends and families. That said, Thanksgiving on a US Navy ship is by no means a poor substitute. The spread is unbelievable; many Sailors swear they eat way better on the ship than they do at home.

A couple of days before Thanksgiving rolled around, I checked the training schedule and saw that on the holiday we were scheduled to perform a fairly light set of exercises, including testing the ship's anchoring systems. Given the relaxed lineup, I asked our OpsO (operations officer) if we could do the exercises close to the base in Coronado, California, where we would once again have cell coverage.

He gave the thumbs-up, so I ran the idea by the admiral. I was slightly concerned he wouldn't agree, given the general intensity of the operations and certification.

"Chopper," he said after I briefed him, "I think it's a great idea. The crew will love it."

On Thanksgiving Day, we headed toward Coronado. When the ship was only a couple of miles from shore, we stopped. My plan was to keep the ship anchored, or "on the hook" as we call it, for three or four hours, enough time for everyone on board to make a call if they wanted. Then I addressed the crew over the 1MC shipwide announcement system.

"Happy Thanksgiving, shipmates. We are now safely anchored off the coast of Coronado, where we're going to stay for the next few hours. Anyone who's not on watch has permission to come to the flight deck and use their cell phone to call home. And if you're on watch, don't worry; we're going to get some relief so you can come up and make a call as well."

Within minutes, the flight deck was teeming with Sailors happily chatting away with their loved ones or posting selfies to social media. It was a fun, special time in the midst of a stressful exercise, and one that made a holiday away from home a bit more pleasant. A few hours later it was all over. We pulled anchor and left to have our Thanksgiving dinner and continue our exercises.

In the panoply of grand gestures, this one barely registered. But having just arrived as CO of the *Theodore Roosevelt*, it was an opportunity for me to set the tone of what our command would be like. In doing so, I received what I believe to be the greatest reward a Navy captain could ask for: I gained the trust and respect of the crew.

~~~~~

One of the strangest things about being the commanding officer in the Navy is that you achieve a certain kind of military celebrity status with the other Sailors on board the ship. Strike up a random conversation with a junior Sailor as you pass them in the hallway and they might well finish the conversation by saying, "I'm going to email my mom and tell her I talked to the captain today!"

It's a humbling experience, but one that helps serve as a reminder of the responsibility that comes with being at the top of a military hierarchical pyramid. And among the many responsibilities inherent in that authority is handing out what we call non-judicial punishment, or NJP for short.

The purpose of NJP is to discipline Sailors for a variety of offenses, usually minor, such as petty theft, destroying government property, sleeping on watch, or disobeying standing orders. It's a long-standing naval tradition built around the idea that the captain is responsible for maintaining order and discipline among the crew while at sea.

This happens during what we call "Captain's Mast," a formal process where the captain hears each NJP case and then acts on it. The captain is both judge and jury. The phrase dates back to the nineteenth century, when most ships had sails. In those days, the captain would hold court under the ship's principal mast (the mainmast) in front of the entire crew. Even after sails and masts became a thing of the past, the name stuck.

As part of Captain's Mast, the captain decides the case, then hands out the punishment. The responsibility is significant . . . as is the opportunity to be a hard-ass. As part of that opportunity, the captain actually has the option to perform Captain's Mast in private or in public (called "open masts"). I've seen many open masts, and in my opinion they're never pretty. In those situations, the captain seems dead-set on making an example of a Sailor or group of Sailors in front of a crowd of several hundred of their peers. It's humiliating, and only serves to kick the crap out of morale.

That's why I always performed Captain's Mast in front of the smallest group of Sailors, chiefs, and officers as possible. Not only did I see the process as a very personal undertaking for the Sailor in question, but I also believed it could be a learning opportunity . . . even though the proceedings often ended with me choosing among several different forms of punishment. I could put a Sailor on restriction. I could demote them. I could take their entire two-week paycheck away from them.

In the most egregious cases, I even had the option of sending Sailors to the brig, the ship's jail (Sailors are typically only confined to the brig if they're felt to be a physical threat to the rest of the crew). In fact, the captain used to be able to go so far as to restrict Sailors to three days of bread and water as part of their time in the brig. Believe it or not, some captains handed out the bread-and-water punishment regularly. In one of the most nefarious cases in recent memory, the captain of a Navy cruiser used it so often that the demoralized crew dubbed the ship the "USS Bread and Water." Thankfully, the practice was outlawed in 2019. I never sent anyone to the brig during my career as a commanding officer, and certainly never even considered bread and water.

Archaic punishments notwithstanding, the justification behind NJP is a good one. With as many as five thousand people aboard a floating city, things are bound to happen, not all of them good. Not surprisingly, the Navy also has a long list of things that its Sailors can and cannot do. Of these, one of the clearest no-nos is drugs. It might be legal in some states, but consuming illegal drugs is strictly forbidden for members of the Navy. In fact, everybody undergoes random drug tests at least twice a year.

One of the first cases I ever adjudicated during Captain's Mast was that of a young Sailor who had tested positive for THC (tetrahydrocannabinol), the active ingredient in marijuana. We call it testing positive, or "popping positive."

Under normal circumstances, the decision is a no-brainer. If you pop positive, you're dismissed from the Navy and your military career comes to an end, obviously with a less-than-perfect record. Most of the time, it's hard to refute the evidence. In fact, pop-positive cases are usually so clear-cut that many commanding officers won't even do Captain's Mast for them and the Sailor is simply dismissed.

I never took that approach, even with Sailors who popped positive. Instead I viewed them as a learning opportunity for everyone involved. A zero-strikes policy could lose a good Sailor.

"Okay, shipmate," I'd say. "If we're going to learn from our mistakes, I need you to be honest about what happened and what you can do better. If I can tell you're lying, then we're not going to learn from this, and my punishment is going to be harsher.

"But remember that I don't have a lot of leeway in pot-positive cases, because the Navy's policy is clear," I'd continue. "If you test positive, then you're supposed to be separated from the Navy, no matter what I want to do."

Their responses usually struck a common chord: they went back home, got together with friends, and fell into old habits. Or they were at a party, drank too much, and one thing led to another. Sailors found guilty could appeal the decision and seek reinstatement, but 99 percent of them never did because they knew they were in the wrong and just wanted out of the Navy at that point.

Yet as clear-cut as positive drug cases may have been, I never found them easy. After all, the decision would have a significant impact on the Sailors' lives going forward. I knew these were not evil people who acted out of malice or wanted to harm the Navy. They had simply made a mistake.

We called the case to order. Before the Sailor came before me, one of the ship's attorneys (a Navy judge advocate general [JAG] and lieutenant commander) approached me.

"Captain," he said, "we don't even have to bother with mast for this case. She popped positive, so you can just sign the papers and we can process her out."

I shook my head. "Let's hear what she has to say."

It was an intimidating scene for anyone. I stood at a podium, flanked on either side by the ship's legal officers, a counselor, a chaplain, and several others from the Sailor's chain of command. It was hardly a private affair, but far fewer than the hundreds of Sailors who could otherwise attend an open mast.

"Shipmate," I began, "you've tested positive for drugs. I don't have a lot of leeway here, but I'd like to hear your side of the story."

In all honesty, I was half-expecting a tale like the ones I usually heard. But this case was different.

This Sailor was married with two young children at home and was the sole breadwinner for the family. Not only that, but her husband was suffering from a fairly aggressive form of cancer and caring for their children while going through chemotherapy back in San Diego. It was a challenging time for the entire family. He couldn't hold down a job given the circumstances, and she was often at sea and hundreds of miles away.

To help alleviate some of the symptoms of the chemotherapy, her husband had been prescribed cannabis products.

"Sir," she said, "I don't smoke pot. However, my husband has these cannabis products in the house, and I'm sure I inadvertently ate or exposed myself to something the last time I was home on leave and taking care of him. I should have been more careful."

She was fighting back tears the entire time, and it was obvious how gut-wrenching the situation was for her. She obviously knew her fate was hanging in the balance, but she owned it and was ready to accept the consequences of her mistake.

For my part, I could have simply followed protocol and dismissed her from the Navy, irrespective of her story. But the facts of the case struck a chord with me, so I asked my legal advisor to explain my options.

"Well, sir," she said, "in addition to the positive test results, she's essentially admitting guilt. And if you find her guilty, then we have to begin the process to separate her from the Navy. But if you really think the exposure was accidental, then we can forgive her. You'll have to write a strong letter to the Navy explaining why you made the decision, because they already have her test results."

Navy policy or not, I knew then that I couldn't dismiss the Sailor in good conscience. Here was a woman who had put her life on the line to serve her country, all while her husband was suffering with cancer back home.

So I didn't.

I found her not guilty by reason of innocent exposure to THC products and wrote a letter explaining my reasons. After a long delay, senior Navy officials back in Washington, DC, accepted my reasons and she was allowed to remain in the Navy.

Afterward, the reaction from the crew members who knew the Sailor was remarkable. At every turn, I was stopped by folks who were aware of the situation and thanked me for excusing her. By acting with compassion and understanding, I showed them I would always have their backs when I could, which helped build a keen sense of trust and mutual respect.

As for the Sailor, she was more dedicated to the ship and the Navy than ever and received nothing but glowing reports from her chain of command thereafter. If she learned anything from the experience, I hope it was that a little kindness can go an awfully long way.

Grim though it may be, life in the military is ultimately about preparing to go into combat. When the bullets are flying and the bombs are dropping, the only reason you're going to stand up to your adversaries is that you've created a bond with the person beside you. And if you're their leader, the only reason they're going to follow you is that they know you'll always have their back. And there's no better way to cement that knowledge than through a little old-fashioned kindness.

CHAPTER 4

Focus on the Closest Alligator

I'd love to say I coined the phrase "Keep the main thing the main thing," but I can't. That distinction goes to the late Stephen Covey, the American author and speaker who wrote *The 7 Habits of Highly Effective People* (Covey's exact quote was "The main thing is to keep the main thing the main thing"). But while the phrase may not be mine, I happily tried to adopt it into the fabric of my personal and professional life, and it served me well from California to the Middle East, and everywhere in between.

In the world of Navy fighter pilots—where situations can change on a moment's notice—we've taken liberties with Covey's saying and modified it so it's a bit more relevant to our profession. The message is the same, but the visual is vastly different: "Always focus on the alligator closest to the canoe." The assumption here is that any alligator near the canoe can

be a life-or-death threat, but the closest one is your greatest
priority at any given time. (Not to be left out, other branches
of the military often say, "Always focus on the wolf closest to
the sled.")

When flying, this means that if there are several things going
on—and there are *always* several things going on during a flight—
you start by prioritizing the closest (and therefore biggest) threat.
For example, if I'm low on fuel and the only safe place to land is
on an aircraft carrier, I tune out every other aspect of the mission
to that point and focus on nothing but a smooth landing before
running out of gas.

We use this saying outside of flight operations as well. If there
are many competing priorities ashore—emails to answer, briefs
to deliver, or budgets to manage—you might hear someone say,
"There's a lot we have to do, but let's start by focusing on the
closest alligator." (And that is *never* answering frivolous emails.)
Once the closest alligator is taken care of, you can then move on
to the next-closest one, and so on.

This is especially important today, where life seems more frag-
mented than ever. In a world of lightning-fast communications,
cell phones that never seem to leave our sides, and astoundingly
short attention spans, there is *always* someone or something
trying to grab our attention. With so many choices and so many
distractions, how do we get the job done? That's where alligators
come into play.

Focusing on the closest alligator is about learning how to
prioritize, and figuring out what's important in your life at any
given moment. Of course, a big part of this is work. Whether
you're employed by a large corporation, a small company, or

even yourself, you are most effective—and most valuable to your employer—when you can see the big picture and address those tasks that are most vital at any given moment.

Alligators certainly don't end there. Your personal life is about prioritizing as well. On any given weekend, you might feel like you've got a thousand things to get done, from cleaning and laundry, to seeing friends and family. If you're not careful and don't prioritize beforehand, you're likely to get to Monday morning and realize that while you were busy all weekend, you didn't actually accomplish anything. It's a subtle distinction, but an important one.

Another analogy I like to use—which I learned early in my career—is that of a glass jar. In this case, the jar represents your life, and your challenge is to fill the jar completely with the contents of three containers set before you. One container holds a series of larger rocks, the second one pebbles, while the third is full of sand. The big rocks represent the most important things in your life, however you define them. The pebbles are less important, and are followed by the sand, which represents the least important—though usually most numerous—tasks in your life.

According to the theory, if you start with the sand and pebbles, you will fill your jar but there will be no room left for the big rocks, the things that really matter.

If you prioritize correctly, on the other hand, you start by putting all your large rocks in the jar. Once that's done, you add the pebbles, which fall between the nooks and crannies left by the rocks. When that's done, then you can turn your attention to the sand, those minuscule, task-related things that chew up your time but mean very little in the long run. The sand will find the even smaller cracks between the rocks and pebbles, eventually filling all the empty spaces.

The glass jar of your life will once again be full, only this time you've prioritized the things you want. Most importantly, if you run out of space, at least you've got the big stuff done.

As captain of a $10 billion aircraft carrier, it was easy to get bogged down by the hundreds of daily decisions and tasks that needed to be made and accomplished to keep the ship running smoothly. And while each of them seemed important in its own right, it was absolutely incumbent to look at the bigger picture, those overarching goals that would ultimately define the strength of my command.

For me, that meant spending considerable time focusing on the long term. What's our operational schedule for the next twelve months? Will the ship need to undergo maintenance later this year? What do the next five years look like? Which strategic decisions do I need to make to ensure the crew's overall well-being and effectiveness, knowing that most of my Sailors and officers will be focused on the immediate tasks at hand?

In my experience, stepping back and taking that big-picture view of life is what allowed me to get the most out of any situation I found myself in, no matter how mundane or challenging. Whether I was navigating a thousand-foot aircraft carrier through crowded waters of Da Nang Harbor in Vietnam, landing an F/A-18 fighter jet on the pitching deck of an aircraft carrier in the black of night, searching for enemies in combat, or battling a pandemic that nobody had ever seen before, I was confident and comfortable leading the Sailors around me because I knew I was focused on the closest alligator in the water.

The importance of prioritizing is drilled into the heads of Navy pilots from the outset of their flying careers. From the first days in flight school, we're taught an important strategy to help maintain laser focus as we prepare to sit in the cockpit of some of the most dangerous and complex machines ever built. We call it "the bubble."

When we're in the bubble, pilots try to tune out *everything* in their heads other than the mission at hand. Your broken-down car, your finances, your family, other job responsibilities, doctor's appointments, pets, world news, sports, romance . . . it all goes out the window and is summarily ignored. In fact, most pilots incorporate the bubble so well into their lives that even our spouses marvel at our ability to compartmentalize and shut out the noise of the everyday. That's not always a valuable trait, particularly when it means you're tuning out important parts of your personal life that are otherwise important to everyday life. I can remember many occasions where Mary told me about a significant event in the life of one of my Navy friends, only to realize that I had learned this information long before, but forgot to share it because I had heard it when I was in my bubble. Needless to say, we pilots aren't always considered the best communicators on the planet . . . at least by our spouses. On the other hand, being able to ignore the white noise of the everyday just might be the most important thing a Navy pilot can do before he or she takes off.

For good reason. The cockpit of an F/A-18 is a formidable environment. In addition to the control stick and throttles, there are dozens of instrument gauges and switches, along with three distinct computer screens that allow a fighter pilot to operate a radar, select a weapon, and use what we call the FLIR (forward-looking infrared) camera to find a target, manage gas reserves, and navigate through friendly or enemy airspace. All of this has to be controlled almost subconsciously, as you fly in formation with other airplanes, or maneuver close to the ground at more than 500 miles per hour. Make a mistake—or take too long to make a decision—and the consequences could be dire, especially when you're in combat or landing on an aircraft carrier.

In those final critical moments, there's no room for error, so the last thing you want to do is commit the slightest bit of attention to anything other than the task at hand. You're focused like you've never been focused before, because your life—as well as the lives of those around you—literally hangs in the balance.

The bubble doesn't solely exist for the duration of the flight, either. It starts with the preflight mission brief, and doesn't end until the postflight debrief is complete. So even though the flight itself may only be an hour, a pilot might ideally be in his or her bubble for as long as five or six hours, sometimes more.

In fact, the pilot's bubble is so respected in the Navy that once you're in it, nobody should bother you with anything that might take your mind away from the task at hand. Even as a very junior pilot, I was given the freedom to turn down requests from my most senior officers.

"Hey, Chopper, can you take care of this admin stuff for me?"

"Sorry, sir, I'm getting ready to fly and I'm in my bubble."

"No problem, I'll go find somebody else to do it."

As venerated as the bubble may be, some officers will

occasionally ignore it . . . much to the consternation of their pilots. In one particularly memorable case, the CO of a squadron radioed one of his pilots (call sign Cage) as Cage was actually sitting in the cockpit, preparing to take off on a training flight.

"Cage, we've made a change to your deployment schedule," the captain said. "Instead of flying out to the ship in three days, we're going to have you walk on board tomorrow evening, before the ship pulls out."

This may not seem like a big deal at first, but it was monumental for Cage. The last-minute schedule change meant that instead of having seventy-two hours to finish his preparations for an extended overseas deployment, he now had mere hours to pack, say goodbye to his wife and kids, and sort through the dozens of other small tasks that needed his attention before shipping off for up to eight months. On top of that, he was just about to take off in an F/A-18 on a training mission. Understandably, he was livid with the CO's timing.

As Cage told me afterward, it was almost impossible for him to think about anything else during the flight. He was angry about the timing of his departure for the deployment, for sure, but even more upset with the way the information was shared. As a result, his safety—as well as the safety of everyone around him—was compromised, and he got little out of the training flight. Luckily, Cage is a great pilot and was able to overcome the distraction. A younger, more inexperienced pilot might have made a crucial mistake while airborne if placed in the same situation.

I understand that the squadron CO likely had a million other things going on and was just trying to check things off his list. But in that case he not only endangered his pilot, he also missed an important opportunity to model sound leadership skills. Believe it or not, Cage still clearly recalled the incident some fifteen years later, albeit with much more humor after all that time had passed.

As I rose in rank during my career and moved from commanding a squadron to commanding ships, I tried to apply the concept of the pilot's bubble to the entire vessel and her crew of hundreds or thousands. It wasn't always easy. A ship doesn't move very quickly, and as a result, Sailors often feel like they've got the luxury of time to make things happen—which often means more opportunity to be distracted from the main thing. My goal as commanding officer was to bring a sense of priority to my crew that had everyone focused on our primary goal at any given moment.

So, just as I had been taught by my best squadron leaders, I passed the pilot's bubble on to the Sailors and officers around me so that it eventually became a vital part of our culture. For me, that meant helping the crew get all the big rocks into our collective bucket first. Whether they were a junior helmsman at the steering wheel of an aircraft carrier in international waters or standing watch in the control tower overseeing the fast-paced operations on the deck below for the first time, the message was always the same: don't be distracted by the little things that are fighting to take your focus from the main thing right now.

In one case, we were preparing to pull into Guam with the USS *Theodore Roosevelt* after an extended period at sea. At the end of my brief to the *Roosevelt*'s crew (which I did almost every day over the ship's 1MC public address system), I took the time to remind everyone of our priority that day.

"Shipmates," I'd say, "we've been at sea for a month and a half and few of us have been able to talk to our friends and family during that time. I know that as soon as we get close to shore and get cell service again that all our phones are going to start going off like crazy with texts and voice mails.

"But we've been entrusted by the Navy to operate this multibillion-dollar aircraft carrier, and our first priority today is to get it safely pierside. And there's a whole lotta currents and boat traffic between us and the port. So until all the last lines are over, the brows [gangplanks] secured, and we're safely tied to the pier, our mission is not over. That is our main thing.

"I don't want you to be distracted thinking about your liberty plans, the meal that's waiting for you, or calling home to talk to your family. They want nothing more than for us to finish this underway period safely, and they'll be there when we're done. And when we're done, then you can put your feet up in your hotel, have a beer, and share all the sea stories you want. But until we've completed our mission, none of that matters."

The power of prioritizing extends to other professional settings as well. Everyone benefits when they can keep their eye on the prize and let the distractions fall away. Think about your typical office environment. In any given workweek there are probably eighty hours of work, but only forty hours to get them done. The way I see it, two things can happen. First, you can manage to check everything off your list and get it all "done," but with 50 percent effort and 50 percent effectiveness. On the other hand, you can sort your rocks, figure out the most important things on your list, and do those really well.

The same principles can actually be applied to family life, too. The stresses of work and professional responsibilities can be difficult for all of us, no matter what kind of job we have. As a Navy captain, my responsibilities were often legion. There was always something else to take care of, always another call that needed to be made, always another email to respond to, no matter what time of the day or day of the week. If I wasn't careful, the job could easily have consumed me.

~~~

When she was commissioned in November 1970, the USS *Blue Ridge* was said to boast the world's most sophisticated electronics and computer suite, one that made her the most advanced joint amphibious command and control center ever constructed. Almost fifty years later, she had undergone enough upgrades to maintain her status as the world's most capable command and control ship.

Yet when I was named CO, the *Blue Ridge* was a far cry from her storied history. The ship was sitting on blocks, out of the water, in Yokosuka, Japan, where she had been undergoing maintenance for the previous sixteen months. Her majestic hull was peppered with gaps and holes; the sounds of grinding metal and blowtorches filled the air. Even the ship's two boilers—her main propulsion system—had been stripped completely and were being rebuilt.

As captain, my task was to get the ship and her crew seaworthy once again. I knew it would be at least another twelve months before maintenance was complete, and overseeing that undertaking was a big part of my responsibilities. Equally important, however, was preparing myself and the rest of the crew for that moment when we left the pier for the first time.

To complicate the issue, some 80 percent of the crew had never been deployed on the *Blue Ridge*, and more than half of them had never been to sea at all. Ever. It's one thing to be pierside and know in theory how a ship works. But it's another thing entirely when you're operating in open water, potentially in the midst of enemies. As CO, I had to consider the immediate tasks at hand with respect to the ship's overhaul, but also look twelve months into the future and consider what we needed to do to get her safely back to sea.

So I set our collective vision. One year into the future, the *Blue Ridge* would once again be steaming safely and confidently around the West Pacific, leading the US Navy's Seventh Fleet. That was our big rock. That was the main thing.

Without such a goal, it would have been much too easy to get lost in the minutiae of our day-to-day work. Without a main thing, we would have forgotten why we were rebuilding the boilers or welding new plates of steel onto the *Blue Ridge*'s hull. But if I could paint that picture for the crew, make them realize that the sum of our collective efforts was to get the ship back to sea, then there would be a method to our madness.

Along the way, I was mindful of the fact that in a huge organization like the Navy, there are thousands of things that anybody could be doing at any time, many of which had absolutely nothing to do with our ultimate goal of getting the *Blue Ridge* back to sea. I knew that if I wasn't careful, the sum effect of those distractions could be disastrous. Even though I had six hundred people working for me on board the ship, those numbers meant nothing unless we were all focused on the same golden ring.

A big part of this was training the rookie crew. I made a point of taking the "bridge teams"—the Sailors and officers ultimately responsible for driving the ship—from the main control station of the ship to the simulator buildings on base for hours on end. Not long before, accidents involving two Navy warships—USS *Fitzgerald* and USS *John S. McCain*—had sadly claimed the lives of seventeen Sailors in the western Pacific, so I considered it paramount that the *Blue Ridge* bridge teams be as competent as possible. And when the simulators weren't available in Japan, we flew to San Diego to use the ones there. By the time the year drew to a close, the bridge teams of the *Blue Ridge* had spent more time in simulators than any Navy crew had done in the previous ten years.

Understandably, I got pushback from some of the other senior leaders on the ship, who were constantly losing their junior officers to other jobs as we set off time and time again for simulator training.

"Captain, we need these Sailors for other jobs, too," they'd say. "They're spending so much time with you, they're falling behind in their other work."

"I realize that . . . and I apologize for the inconvenience," I'd reply. "But for now, I need you to make do and live without them from time to time. I realize this is going to come at a cost, and I know it's going to mean that some of their other work will be a little bit behind. But in the end, learning to drive this ship safely is the single most important thing these Sailors can do right now."

Even the future officers of the deck themselves—relatively junior division officers who would be responsible for the safe navigation of the ship—felt the effects of the intense training we put them through. Here they were spending all their spare time in simulators, even as they were trying to keep up with the dozens of things they needed to learn as part of their jobs as newly commissioned officers.

"I understand that all those other things are important, because I had to learn how to do them, too," I'd tell them. "And I want you to be a good, well-rounded officer, but for now you have to focus on learning how to drive this ship. Believe me, you'll get good at paperwork. But right now, this is our priority."

And that's exactly what happened. They might have fallen behind slightly on some of their administrative work, for sure. I was okay with that. I accepted the fact that we weren't going to be great in some areas, because I wanted us to be great in the one area that *really* mattered. So by establishing our priorities and making them clear to everyone involved, our bridge teams became the best damned group of ship drivers a captain could ask for. It was a comforting feeling. As commanding officer, I never had the luxury of spending all my time on the deck driving the ship, and having strong, confident, and competent bridge teams meant I could focus on my other responsibilities.

As those final twelve months drew to a close, the reality of our efforts started to take shape. Thanks to a ton of work and consistent reminders of our collective goal, we all began to recognize that we were getting very close to achieving our vision of getting the *Blue Ridge* safely back to sea.

In the last few days before we left the pier and got under way for the first time, the activity level on the ship reached a frantic pace. Once again, I addressed the crew over the 1MC.

"Shipmates," I said, "as we prepare to take in all the lines and get the *Blue Ridge* under way in forty-eight hours, there are going to be dozens of things battling for your attention. But if they are not related to getting this ship safely to sea, you have my authority to unequivocally say no to them.

"If the base calls and asks you to update the parking plan for the crew, you tell them they're going to have to wait a few days. If the admiral's staff tells you they need those forms submitted ASAP, you tell them on my authority that it won't be coming anytime soon. And rest assured I will back you up on those decisions, no matter what."

I imagine they appreciated hearing it, because they knew I would have their backs. What I didn't tell them, however, was just how much was at stake. With the tragic accidents involving the *McCain* and the *Fitzgerald* having happened just twelve months before, I knew the eyes of the Navy were on us. If we got the ship under way and had an accident, then none of the work we had done over the previous two years would matter; people would still only remember the fact that we, too, had messed up.

Finally, the day arrived, and we were set to get the USS *Blue Ridge* under way. Our goal was simple: navigate safely through Tokyo Bay to open water, where we would engage in what we call sea trials, a series of tests on every system and piece of equipment on board the ship. Five days later, we would return the ship safely to base.

Under normal circumstances, the commander of the Seventh Fleet—a Navy vice admiral—and his or her entire staff would be on board the *Blue Ridge*. After all, that is a Navy command ship's raison d'être: provide command, control, communications, and intelligence support to the fleet via its commander. In this case, the fleet commander and I had initially decided that he and his staff of 350 would stay behind during our initial sea trials, which would allow me and the rest of the crew to focus on the task at hand.

Yet due to some unforeseen schedule changes, the admiral changed his mind shortly before we were set to leave port. He was new to the position and eager to get his staff settled on board. In all fairness, I could relate to his sense of urgency: the *Blue Ridge* had been delayed in maintenance, and everyone had been waiting to get back to sea for a long time. I wasn't 100 percent comfortable with the idea, but I knew the crew was ready. So the admiral and his staff came on board.

I'd like to say it wasn't a distraction . . . but it was. Now, in addition to focusing on our main thing, we also had to worry about accommodating the fleet commander, his senior officers, and their staff of hundreds. A big part of that was ensuring that the sophisticated electronics and computer systems that run the fleet were functional. Of course, I knew we could do both. But at the same time, I wanted to make sure the admiral and I were on the same page about our priorities.

"Sir," I said, "we're happy to have you and your staff on board. But our main thing hasn't changed: safely getting the ship to sea, running our sea trials, and safely returning."

"That makes total sense, Chopper," he replied. "I appreciate you being so accommodating, and I agree one hundred percent with your priorities."

Serendipitously enough, the admiral was called back to Washington a few days before we were set to get under way and never made the trip. His staff, however, remained on board. Suddenly our communication and computer systems became even more important, as the admiral's staff needed to be in nearly constant contact with their boss.

A few hours later, we set off. All things considered, our departure from the pier was an unadulterated success. The bridge team marveled at how easy it was to drive the ship after countless hours of simulator time, and expertly navigated us through Tokyo Bay and around the southern island of Japan, where we started our sea trials.

Predictably, not everything ran smoothly, and some of our air-conditioning systems began to fail on our first day out. The Sailors and I could handle a bit of discomfort, but the AC was also used to cool our mainframe computers and communications systems. And while these systems weren't necessary to safely operate the ship, they were vital to the fleet commander's staff.

Nevertheless, when the air conditioners started to fail we had no choice but to shut down some of our computer and communications systems, which meant a loss of connectivity back to the base. Suddenly the admiral's staff became very worried about not being able to do their jobs. So when one of his senior officers showed up on the bridge as the sun was setting that evening, I assumed what he was going to say.

"Captain," he told me, "this isn't going to work for us. We need to talk about pulling back into base until this is sorted out."

I empathized with his position. At the same time, though, I wasn't having any of it.

"I understand where you're coming from," I replied. "But you have to remember that this is the first time the *Blue Ridge* has been under way in twenty-eight months, and we knew things like this would likely happen. And now you want me to head back to

Tokyo and navigate through the busiest waterway in the Pacific *at night* with a crew that has never driven this ship before?

"I won't let that happen," I continued. "At least not now. If you want to come talk to me tomorrow morning when it makes more sense, that's fine. I'm happy to get close to shore so maybe you have some phone connectivity. But I'm not going to pull back in pierside in the dead of night.

"I'm doing this as a favor to you, too, because in the last year the Navy has crashed two ships out here. And I'm not going to put the ship in a situation where there's a risk that could happen again."

The admiral's staff accepted my decision. I think in the end they understood that our top priority at the moment was to operate safely at sea and finish our sea trials. To his credit, the admiral understood that, and had agreed to it a long time before.

For me, it was equally important that I keep my word to my crew. I had been telling them for the better part of a year that the closest alligator was to operate the *Blue Ridge* safely at sea. I would have been a complete hypocrite if I suddenly turned around and said we were going to assume an otherwise unacceptable level of risk to pull the ship back in at night just to take care of the admiral's staff. They would never have trusted me again . . . and for good reason.

In the end, we stayed at sea for the duration of our sea trials and returned safely to Yokosuka Harbor. Once again, the *Blue Ridge* crew expertly navigated the traffic of one of the world's busiest waterways and brought the ship safely to the pier without incident. As for the fleet commander's staff, they somehow managed to make it through those five days without the world coming to a grinding halt. And through it all, we kept our main thing our main thing.

~~~~~

A *Nimitz*-class US naval aircraft carrier is one of the most imposing machines ever constructed. At 1,092 feet long and weighing more than 100,000 tons, she can reach top speeds of over 30 knots (35 mph), thanks to two nuclear reactors that generate approximately 260,000 horsepower. In 2018, the approximate cost to build one of these behemoths was nearly $10 billion.

A typical aircraft carrier accommodates an airwing of more than fifty F/A-18 fighter jets, more than a dozen helicopters, and numerous radar and logistic aircraft. Add to this a host of short-range defensive weaponry for antiaircraft warfare, a complex missile defense system, and a total crew of trained military personnel numbering five thousand strong and you've got the recipe for one of the world's most formidable vessels.

While a carrier's nuclear reactors will theoretically keep her running indefinitely, its food and other supplies are finite, which means the ship has to be restocked regularly. Since pulling into port is usually not an option, we resupply our ships at sea through a process we call underway replenishment. To make the exercise even more complex, we do it *while moving*. That may not seem like a problem if you're in two canoes in the calm waters of your local lake. But do it with two massive ships in the middle of the world's biggest oceans, where wind, tides, and waves as high as twenty-five feet come together at nature's whim, and the potential for error is very real.

Despite the inherent risks, the rationale for underway

replenishment is sound. The alternative is to establish a network of refueling and restocking stations around the world. During times of conflict, this infrastructure would be extremely vulnerable to disruption or attack. What's more, regular use of such stations would introduce a predictable pattern to naval operations that enemies could easily exploit. Underway replenishment keeps the Navy agile, unpredictable, and self-sufficient.

The concept of underway replenishment actually dates back to the early 1900s, primarily through the efforts of the British Royal Navy. In the US Navy, the concept was perfected by legendary American naval admiral Chester W. Nimitz, who was working as the XO on the USS *Maumee* in 1916. The *Maumee* was what we call an oiler, a combat logistics ship that replenished other vessels with fuel, food, munitions, and other necessities.

When World War I started, Nimitz recognized that the most efficient way to supply other Navy ships from the *Maumee* was to pull alongside them. Coming to a dead stop would have made both ships vulnerable to enemy planes, submarines, and ships, along with unpredictable sea conditions. By maintaining speed alongside one another, the two ships could continue to navigate around these many potential risk factors while simultaneously minimizing the risk of accidentally colliding with one another.

The process of underway replenishment—which we often call "unrep"—has evolved since Nimitz's time, but the concept and the risks are the same. Today we transfer millions of gallons of jet fuel and tens of thousands of pounds of food, equipment, bombs, ammunition, and other supplies in a matter of hours. The process is intense, and the stakes are high. If the crews become distracted from their mission, the results could be disastrous.

The process begins with the supply ship—itself a massive vessel measuring some six hundred feet long—maintaining a set course and speed of approximately 13 knots (15 mph). Then it's the responsibility of the aircraft carrier to maneuver alongside and match the supply ship's speed and bearing. The two ships need to be approximately 180 feet apart for the exercise to be successful. That might seem like a lot of wiggle room, but it's actually very tight considering the size of the vessels. Turn either ship just one or two degrees the wrong way, and they may collide or pull apart, potentially causing millions of dollars' worth of damage . . . or worse.

The evening before the process begins, we hold a ship-wide briefing where all the watchstanders—key people in various positions during an evolution—discuss their role in the exercise. The operations officer talks about the schedule, the navigator discusses the course, the officer of the deck explains the approach, the intelligence officers bring everyone up to speed on potential threats, and the young Sailors who are actually steering the ship and monitoring the backup equipment discuss their procedures and responsibilities.

As commanding officer, my job was to oversee the entire process. So when it was finally my turn to speak (the captain always goes last), my message usually rang a common tone. "Let's remember that our primary responsibility is to get this done as safely and smoothly as possible," I'd say. "That's our main thing."

When the ships are parallel and in sync, the aircraft carrier shoots a series of lines to the supply ship to initiate the connection process. It's an incredible sight: gunner mates and bosun mates with exceptional aim line up along the deck of the carrier and use M14 rifles to launch lines with baseball-sized rubber bullets across the open ocean to waiting crew members on the supply ship. The lines get progressively bigger until the two ships are eventually connected through a series of thick, high-tension steel cables.

Once the two ships are connected and secured, the supply ship uses forklifts and a hydraulic lift system (think of the world's most expensive zip line) to load pallets of supplies onto the cables and send them across the open ocean to crew members waiting on the carrier. When that's done, a series of high-pressure fuel lines are connected, and the carrier will take on as much as 1.5 million gallons of jet fuel in just a couple of hours. To put this in perspective, consider that the pump at your local gas station pumps at about 10 gallons of gasoline per minute. To transfer 1.5 million gallons of fuel at that rate would take 104 consecutive days, working twenty-four hours a day.

Given the value of goods being transferred and the complexity of the undertaking, we have to get it right. The two ships are uncomfortably close to one another on the open ocean, with an incredible amount of pressure on the cables that connect them. If the seas are calm, it's a fairly straightforward undertaking, particularly because the Sailors on both vessels are exceptionally well trained. But when the seas are heavy or there's a need to navigate around obstacles or potential threats, it can be nerve-racking.

Luckily, we train our crews for a host of possibilities during underway replenishment, including live combat scenarios. In one certification exercise off the coast of San Diego, the *Theodore Roosevelt* was conducting an underway replenishment while simultaneously launching airplanes from the flight deck and keeping a close eye on an "enemy" submarine fifteen miles away. As part of the exercise, we had to turn the two ships in unison— all while connected and traveling at 13 knots in fifteen-foot seas.

It was an exercise in alligator focus for virtually every member of the crew . . . though admittedly some shouldered greater responsibilities than others. On the bridge, the "lee helmsman" jockeyed the throttles to add or subtract an RPM from the ship's four twenty-foot-wide propellers, or "screws." At the same time, the helmsman on the ship's steering wheel would carefully change the carrier's course plus or minus half a degree to control our two 30x20-foot rudders and keep the two ships at the desired 180-foot separation.

In the tower, the air boss—the senior person in the tower who monitors the flight deck—and his team had one priority: overseeing the helicopter and jet flight operations taking place throughout the operation. On the radar and navigation charts, the quartermasters and operation specialists focused on one thing only: the safe navigation of the carrier around the last known location of the enemy submarine. In fact, the only person charged with thinking about more than one thing was me. As captain, I was accountable for all of it.

It wasn't always easy to stay focused. Even during underway replenishment, emails still came in and the phone and radio still rang. Sailors still got sick, plans had to be made, questions needed to be answered. But I never allowed myself to get distracted during those six or eight hours, because I knew I had to keep focused on the main thing. Except for the occasional quick bathroom break, everything else was on hold.

Someone once said that a good leader doesn't just set

priorities, but simplifies those priorities as well. For me, that meant that if I did my job correctly, I could approach any Sailor during a mission and they would understand their specific job as well as our main thing at that time. I knew that to be a good leader, my job was to simplify and clarify our goals to the point where *everyone* on board was focused on the main thing, and their role in making that vision a reality.

Keeping the main thing the main thing, focusing on the closest alligator, putting the big rocks in the jar . . . in the end they all sound a bit like glorified bumper stickers. But it's the execution that makes all the difference. Few of us will ever find ourselves defending a canoe from fearsome reptiles, flying combat missions in an F/A-18, or doing all we can to protect thousands of people under our charge from a deadly virus. But that doesn't mean we can't learn to take a step back from the everyday noise of our lives and allow ourselves the opportunity to set our priorities for that day, week, month, or year, whether we're sitting at our desks at work or simply kicking back on a Friday night and deciding what the weekend holds.

CHAPTER 5

Pull Like a Clydesdale

As a general rule, Navy chiefs are a salty bunch . . . and for good reason. Not a single one has been given a free ticket or an easy ride to get where they are. They've worked their butts off over the years, seen just about everything a person could imagine, and fought tooth and nail for every advancement they've made. So when a chief speaks, you listen.

Senior Chief Jeff Foresman was no exception. He was Chief Damage Controlman (DC Chief) on the USS *Ronald Reagan*, the senior person in charge of the ship's damage control program. His responsibilities were many and varied, and included everything related to emergency services: fire prevention, firefighting, and damage control; even things like chemical, biological, and radiological warfare defense. Senior Foresman had not only seen some stuff through his career, but he had risen through the ranks to the point where he was directly in charge of a team of one hundred Sailors, and responsible for the firefighting training of all five thousand Sailors on board. He was an exceptionally quiet and matter-of-fact man, so when he actually had something to say, my ears perked up . . . even if sometimes I wasn't sure if he was pulling my leg or not.

"Hey, XO," he said one day as we sat in Damage Control Central, the room that's used to monitor the status of the entire ship—including things like flooding, fire, list control, and nuclear reactor status. "How much weight do you think a Clydesdale can pull?"

"I don't know, Senior," I replied. "Five thousand pounds."

"You're pretty close, sir," he said. "It's somewhere between two thousand and eight thousand, but no more than eight thousand pounds, max. Now, how much weight can a team of two Clydesdales pull?"

I wasn't sure what he was getting at, but I played along. "I'm gonna go with somewhere between four thousand and sixteen thousand pounds, but sixteen tops."

"Wrong," he said. "When they work together, two Clydesdales can pull twenty-four thousand pounds. And if properly trained, that goes up to thirty-two thousand pounds."

"The math doesn't work."

"Sure it does, sir," he said. With that he stood up and walked away, leaving me to chew on the little nugget he had shared with me.

Senior Chief never spoke with me about it again. Thanks to the power of the internet, I have since been able to corroborate Senior Chief Foresman's story. At the time, though, it was the essence of what he said that resonated so deeply with me, if only because it echoed what I had learned on the ballfields as a kid and continued to relearn—whether airborne or at sea—throughout my career: we are stronger when we pull together.

Whether you're in the military or not, you can get a lot more done as part of a team than by yourself. Assemble a group of people who understand their collective goal, the importance of what they're doing, and each person's value to the organization, and there's no limit to what can be accomplished.

~~~~~~

It should come as little surprise to anyone that in the military we *love* rank. But what most people don't know is that there are several tracks to becoming an officer, no matter which branch of service you are in. Most officers must earn a four-year college degree before entering the military, and have gone through a specialized military channel, either Reserve Officers' Training Corps (ROTC), officer candidate school, or a service academy such as the US Naval Academy, in Annapolis, Maryland, where I studied. There are also warrant officers and limited duty officers who were prior enlisted Sailors that become technical experts in their field and were subsequently commissioned as naval officers and given additional leadership responsibilities.

In the military we also have noncommissioned officers, or what we call petty officers in the Navy. Petty officers are all prior enlisted individuals who have no officer training but have worked their way up the ladder through years of service, experience, proven leadership, and successful completion of rigorous, semi-annual advancement exams. They are promoted from within by those who recognize the strength and value they bring to the organization; they get more responsibility and authority as a result. Moving up the ladder as a petty officer isn't easy, but if someone works hard and demonstrates the ability to lead their shipmates, they can advance over time.

Along the way, a petty officer can rise in rank from Petty Officer Third Class (E-4, the lowest rank of petty officer) to Chief Petty Officer (E-7). Chiefs are the Navy's equivalent to middle managers in a business organization, and within the chief ranks you can be promoted all the way to Master Chief Petty Officer (E-9). Almost every department or division has a chief. They are experienced, knowledgeable, and vital to the success of any ship or squadron. As I learned in the winter of 1995, they can also help a young, inexperienced officer learn how to lead, even if he has never done it before.

I joined the Navy to fly. In fact, it was only after I found out that to fly you had to first go to college to be an officer that I applied to the Naval Academy. I got my degree in mathematics and then spent two years in flight school learning how to be a helicopter pilot in Pensacola, Florida. After I earned my wings in Pensacola, I was on my way to Barbers Point, Hawaii. Barbers Point holds a special place in my heart for a number of reasons, not the least of which is that our oldest son, Connor, was born there. The fact that I learned to surf there didn't hurt, either.

When I arrived at Barbers Point, I knew how to fly the Navy's most advanced helicopter at the time (the SH-60B Seahawk), because that's what I'd been trained to do. But I had little real-world leadership training outside of the Academy. In fact, the last real leadership experience I had was as a senior lifeguard back in high school, when I was in charge of five other junior lifeguards. It seemed like a lot of responsibility at the time. I was in for a rude awakening.

On my first day with the Easyriders, I sat down to check in with the XO of the squadron, Commander Karl Kolesnikoff, who—as the number two guy in charge of the squadron—laid out his expectations for then lieutenant Crozier.

"All right, Brett [we didn't have call signs for helicopter pilots back then], I know that you know how to fly a helicopter," he said. "That's extremely important and I want you to continue to refine your skills. But we're going to start giving you leadership responsibilities, too. So we're putting you in charge of the Line Division."

I tried desperately to hide my confusion. What the heck is a Line Division?

"We've also got a big maintenance inspection coming up in a few months that you need to prepare your division for," he added.

And that was it. I had no real idea what a Line Division was, who was on it, or what purpose it served. The Naval Academy had given me some fundamental leadership training during my four years there, but I had rarely applied the training anywhere. In all honesty, I was hoping to spend time with Mary enjoying Hawaii and work on getting my qualifications as a pilot so I could become a helicopter aircraft commander somewhere down the road. At the same time, I was honored to have been given the responsibility of leading my own division. I decided I would do whatever it took to learn, and started by seeking out the one person the XO said could train me: the chief in the Line Division, Ruben Garcia.

He wasn't easy to find, at least not for a wide-eyed rookie like me. The Line Division at Barbers Point was also called the Line Shack because the division was housed in its own run-down building near the helicopter flight line. Inside the Shack was a small office, where I found Chief Garcia hulking over a desk in the corner of the room.

He was an intimidating fellow, as crusty and salty as they come. Covered in tattoos, Chief Garcia looked like he had been in the Navy for a lifetime and had witnessed things I could only have imagined at that point. In theory, he was working for me since I was an officer and senior in rank, but I still viewed him as just a few steps below God. I called upon what little confidence I had and mustered the courage to speak.

"Good morning, Chief Garcia!" I said a bit too eagerly. "I'm Lieutenant Crozier and I've just been told I'm running the Line Division."

He peered up from what he was doing and sized me up. The Hawaiian heat didn't seem to bother Chief Garcia at all while I stood sweating in the close, humid air of the office. For a moment I thought he was going to growl at me, but his tanned face broke into a smile as he stood up.

"Welcome to the Line Shack," he said as he shook my hand and clapped me warmly on the back with his meaty paw. "We're gonna love having you. I imagine you've got a thousand questions."

"Chief," I said, breathing a sigh of relief now that the tension had been broken, "I've got a *million* questions."

For the next hour, Chief Garcia bombarded me with far more information than I could possibly remember. He had been in the Line Division for the last three years and had mastered every nuance of the business. I tried to scribble notes as he piled books, binders, and papers on the desk in front of me, but 99 percent of what he said flew over my head. Meanwhile, all I kept thinking was *Oh my God ... I just want to go jump in a helicopter and fly because it's the only thing I really know how to do.*

The look of confusion must have been obvious on my face because Chief stopped midsentence and gave me a thoughtful look. Then he gave me advice that stayed with me for the rest of my Navy career.

"I know this seems like a lot," he said. "But here's the deal. As the Line Division officer, you're not gonna be the one out there working on the helicopters. Your job is to take care of the guys who are. And if you can learn how to do that—even if you don't know how to right now—they'll take care of the rest."

I looked at the chief and realized there was more to him than his tattooed-biker appearance suggested. He had been leading Sailors in the Navy for almost as long as I'd even known what the Navy was, and he obviously knew what worked and what didn't.

He continued: "So when the operations officer wants us to run a fourteen-hour schedule and these guys are running ragged, I need you to step up and say, 'Hey, my guys need a break.' And when you see that morale is getting low, you need to be the guy who motivates these Sailors and tells them what a privilege it is to fly the helicopters that they take care of."

"Chief," I said, "I can do that. I know I have a lot to learn, and I will learn it. But I'll start by just making sure I take care of these guys and be their best advocate."

He smiled as he led me out of the office toward the hangar, where he would introduce me to the Sailors I would soon be leading. "The way I see it, you have three primary responsibilities as an officer, and they will stay the same throughout your career."

"What are those?" I asked with curiosity.

"Number one, take care of your Sailors.

"Number two, take care of your Sailors.

"And number three, take care of your Sailors."

In the weeks that followed, I took the chief's advice to heart. The Line Division was a group of about two dozen Sailors responsible for cleaning and servicing the helicopters, like a NASCAR pit crew. It was hot, greasy, sweaty work. And while the people of the Line Shack were still too junior to do serious maintenance on the choppers like rebuilding engines, they did just about everything else; their job was an important one.

I couldn't do what they did. I didn't know how to change hydraulic fluids or service an engine. But I *could* make sure that Line Crew was taken care of. And I did. I stepped up when I thought they were being overworked. I made sure they had everything they needed to do their jobs. And I shared with them how great it was to fly the helicopters they had worked on.

Over time, I could tell they appreciated it. More importantly, I saw firsthand that taking care of their work environment allowed them to do their job to the best of their abilities and enjoy it along the way. Yes, I was senior to them by several pay grades, but I tried never to let that get in the way. We were humans, we were Sailors, and we had a common goal. In fact, the only thing I used my authority as an officer for was to get them what they needed.

A few months after I started, a team from Naval Headquarters in San Diego was scheduled to fly to Barbers Point to perform a complete inspection of the squadron. As part of it, every aspect of the Line Division's performance would be assessed, from hazardous materials' documentation to Sailors' physical fitness.

The inspectors would even go so far as to scour the helicopter flight line for random metal objects that might get sucked into a chopper's million-dollar turbine engines and damage them. It was the first inspection I had to face as a young officer, and I was understandably nervous.

I wanted us to do well. That said, I wasn't going to be the one in the trenches doing all the dirty work to prepare; most of that responsibility fell on the shoulders of my Sailors. My job was to ensure that all the paperwork was in order, and the Sailors were properly trained for their jobs. In the week before the inspection, they busted their butts to get ready, and I felt confident that we were in good shape. Yet as Friday approached, I began to feel pressure from my senior officers that the Line Division needed to work over the upcoming weekend to make sure we were ready for the inspection the following Tuesday.

I certainly had the authority to make everyone come to work. At the same time, I knew it would crush the weekend for my Sailors, who at that point had already been working twelve-hour days in anticipation of the inspection. Not only that, but we were in *Hawaii* for goodness' sake. The Sailors lived for their free time, where they could hang out at the beach, surf, and explore. I was torn, so I sought out the chief and asked his opinion.

"I think you know that the division is ready to go, sir," he said confidently. "So let's take care of our people and give them the weekend off. And if they need to, they'll work extra hard Monday to be ready on Tuesday."

I heeded his advice and gave everyone the weekend off. I'd be lying if I said I wasn't a bit worried that I had made the wrong choice. But the team was ecstatic with the decision and did exactly as the chief had predicted. They appreciated the gesture of trust from me, then doubled their efforts on Monday. And when Tuesday arrived, we performed phenomenally well on the inspection.

For me, it was an opportunity to experience what happens when we take care of people and trust them to respond in kind. My senior officers might have second-guessed my decision at the time, but I felt great knowing that I hadn't ruined the weekend for my Sailors just because I was worried that we wouldn't do well.

Looking back, I think I already knew the importance of taking care of people, but Chief Garcia was the one who reinforced the importance of it as a leader. And as my career advanced and I progressively assumed more authority and responsibility, I never forgot his advice. From the day we met in the Line Shack back in 1995 to the day I was relieved of my duties as commanding officer of the *Theodore Roosevelt*, it was *Take care of your Sailors, take care of your Sailors, take care of your Sailors.* In turn, they will take care of everything else.

~~~~~

During my first few weeks as commanding officer of the USS *Theodore Roosevelt*, the crew and I were put through a series of training operations to demonstrate our readiness for deployment. Following our Thanksgiving Day cell phone break, we sailed farther out to sea for our culminating exercises with the other ships and air squadrons of the carrier strike group.

The exercises were taking place a few hundred miles off the coast of Southern California, in what is known in Navy parlance as *blue water*. Rather than refer to a specific section of ocean, blue water is a general term that's used to describe a situation where an aircraft carrier is operating far enough from shore that the ship is the only safe place for aircraft to take off and land. In naval terms, there is no available divert. In other words, when the crap hits the fan, get back to the ship.

Not surprisingly, blue water operations also require extensive planning. It's not as simple as launching a bunch of fighter jets and knowing they can stop for fuel and/or maintenance at any number of bases along the coast during the course of the mission if necessary. In blue water ops, there are no bases, no airports, no community landing strips. The ship is the beginning and the end. As a result, it's absolutely critical to calculate each jet's range and the amount of time it can stay airborne without running out of fuel, a figure entirely dependent on how the pilot handles the craft and the maneuvers inherent to the mission. Miscalculate by even a little and the consequences can be dire: as technologically advanced and powerful as an F/A-18 may be, it doesn't glide. Without fuel, it plummets into the sea in a matter of seconds.

Despite such risks, the US Navy recognizes that the ability to operate in blue water gives it a unique advantage over the world's other navies, and it is the only navy on earth that can remain fully functional and battle-ready under these circumstances. It makes us exceptionally formidable, but that type of edge doesn't come without risk. In fact, other navies don't regularly operate in blue water because there's a constant (though slim) chance it can end in disaster for airplanes and aircrew alike.

So we acknowledge and accept the risks, then train extensively in the blue water environment, which allows us to master its nuances and become accustomed to its unpredictability. But when you're floating in the middle of the ocean, even when you're expecting the unpredictable, you can still be surprised.

Back in the fall of 2019, we were in the final throes of our blue water training exercises when the seas started to pick up. The swells quickly rose from virtually nothing to over twenty feet, and a wall of dense fog rolled in. It's fairly typical November weather in the Pacific Ocean off the coast of Southern California, and under normal circumstances we maneuver the ship until we find a patch of clear skies, at least one big enough to land the jets. This time, though, there was none to be found.

To make matters worse, we were in the middle of what we call cyclic ops, flight-training operations where the ship is continually landing and launching aircraft. We had just launched twelve jets, with another ten in the air that had been airborne for over an hour and were low on gas and ready to land when the weather went completely sideways. It was an eerie scene for those of us on the ship. The *TR* pitched on the waves; and the fog was so thick it was impossible to catch even a glimpse of any of the F/A-18s, the only indication of their existence the constant drone of the engines as they circled overhead.

For the pilots in the midst of their training missions, it was even more disconcerting. Under normal circumstances, an F/A-18 pilot has to be able to "break out" and see the ship from about a half mile away to be able to safely land on the flight deck. At that point, the pilot "calls the ball," which means he or she lines up the jet's approach with the centerline of the landing area on the flight deck and the ship's Fresnel lens glideslope indicator (the "meatball" or "ball," based on the shape of the light when viewed from the cockpit). Once that's done, the pilot establishes communications with the carrier's landing signal officer (LSO), who helps guide the pilot in for the final critical seconds of the landing. If the pilot can't see the ship clearly and call the ball from a safe distance, the LSO will wave off the airplane by flashing a series of red lights on the flight deck at the jet and have them either circle back around for another attempt or wait for the weather to clear.

This time, though, the weather wasn't clearing. Now we had two dozen planes in the air, half of which had burned through most of their fuel during their training ops and needed to land. Given their fuel levels, they were only going to have a couple of chances to approach the ship and land. Failure spelled disaster.

I watched this unfold from the bridge, scanning our weather radar for a hint of clear sky somewhere close by. The *TR* was cutting through the water at the maximum speed we felt comfortable considering the limited visibility, but still we found no relief. We were smack in the middle of impenetrable fog. Despite all my confidence in my crew's ability, I was quietly beginning to feel real concern for the pilots' safety.

Then, without warning, we lost our entire radio communication system, along with any ability to communicate with the planes in the air. There was no way to update the pilots on our attempts to find better weather, no way for the LSOs to guide them to the flight deck during their final approaches. What had to that point been an "interesting" situation escalated to a serious problem in seconds.

It's not like we were caught completely unprepared. We train extensively in what we call EMCON conditions, where we land planes on aircraft carriers with no radio communication capabilities. But the added variables of the weather, the sea state, and the lack of visibility took the situation to a whole new level. With more than twenty planes in the air, coordination was the key to success. Only now it was impossible. If things didn't change soon, there was a palpable chance we could lose aircraft, aircrew, or both.

There was a very clear sense of urgency on the bridge. But to the infinite credit of everyone involved, nobody panicked. In one of the most compelling displays of teamwork and professionalism I have ever seen, everybody kept their head in the game and started working to address the issue.

I picked up the handheld internal ship radio I used to talk to all the senior officers on board, and as calmly as I could, communicated the situation to the ship's key leaders, asking them to direct their efforts toward the problem at hand. Then the combat systems officer (who was in charge of all our radios) and I started looking into the communications failure. With the help of his team of technicians and radio specialists, and the people in the control tower, he was very quickly able to get the ship's standby radio fully functional. It wasn't perfect, but at least it afforded us the opportunity to communicate with the fighter jets circling overhead. (We would find out later that an electrical short had knocked out the comms system; luckily the backup radio was portable and battery operated.)

With one line of communication open, the *Roosevelt*'s senior air traffic controller stepped in and began to coordinate the jets, calmly but decisively assessing the fuel state of each F/A-18 and directing them to a different holding pattern overhead, all while also keeping the pilots abreast of our efforts to find a break in the weather. In doing so, he was able to prioritize which jets were lowest on fuel and establish a clear landing order once the weather allowed.

Meanwhile, the flight deck crew was as efficient as I had ever seen; they understood that once it became possible to land, the planes would come in quick succession, and they would need to clear the landing area as smoothly and safely as possible to make room for the next plane. We also prepared a series of tanker jets, which could be quickly launched to provide more fuel airborne to those that needed it the most . . . though we knew that every tanker we launched would eventually have to land as well.

With the entire crew now focused on the task at hand, I felt the weight lift slightly off my shoulders. The situation was still bordering on what I call *in extremis*, a high-risk situation where you're operating at the edge of the envelope and the consequences of failure are significant. But we never got there. With the *TR*'s Sailors all working together as a team, I knew we were doing everything possible under the circumstances.

After what seemed like the longest thirty minutes in recorded history, the ship was able to find somewhat clearer skies and we were able to coordinate the landing of the jets. One by one they stretched across the Pacific sky for miles. The first few to touch down were so low on fuel you could see the relief on the pilots' faces as they emerged from the cockpits. The jets hit the flight deck in quick succession, and soon they were all back safely on the *Teddy Roosevelt*.

For me, the experience was one that demonstrated not only the importance of teamwork, but also how leaders need to learn to rely upon their people to achieve true success. There was no way I would have been able to address everything that went wrong that afternoon, and I knew that.

Instead I relied on the strength of the team to solve the problem. I recognized that the people around me were all committed professionals who shared the same goal as me: get the pilots down safely without any loss of life or aircraft. I maintained my faith in their abilities, and everyone stepped up. Only by pulling together as a team—just as Senior Chief Foresman had reminded me so many years earlier—were we able to get everyone back on the ship without any loss of life.

~~~~

One of the reasons a military career (particularly that of a Navy pilot) is attractive to so many people is that—more so than most other professions on earth—it resembles a team sport. From the language and call signs we use to describe our activities (for instance, we always refer to our missions and activities using *we* instead of *I*) to the ready rooms and locker rooms we share when we brief for flights or suit up in our flight gear and helmets, Navy pilots tend to be former athletes, men and women who are as comfortable on the field or court as they are in the air. Because of that background, we're really good at adopting a team mentality and carrying it forward into every aspect of our jobs.

I spent most of my career keenly aware of the fact that I was only one cog in a massive machine that was dependent on each of its parts to function efficiently and successfully. From the youngest cook on the mess deck to the most senior fighter pilot dropping a precision-guided weapon at a critical target in Afghanistan, every job was as important as the next.

It wasn't always easy to stay grounded, though, especially during my heady early days. When I was a student at the Naval Academy, *all* I wanted was to be a Navy pilot. For me it was the MVP position, the focal point of every operation. Little did I realize then that without the efforts of thousands of other people behind the scenes, a helicopter or fighter jet would never even get off the deck of an aircraft carrier.

Even in the air a fighter jet is merely one piece of a very large puzzle. During tactical combat missions, F/A-18s usually fly in divisions of four jets working together, whether the goal is to down enemy aircraft or drop bombs on a target. These divisions are accompanied by E-2 Hawkeye early warning (radar) airplanes, which provide command and control capabilities during our missions. Hawkeyes also provide sea and land surveillance, control fighter jets during air defense operations, control strike aircraft on offensive missions, and even control search-and-rescue efforts for aviators and Sailors lost at sea. Then there are the aircraft charged with electronic attack during tactical missions, the F/A-18G Growlers. Among their many jobs, these planes use advanced electronics to scramble enemy radar systems, so they don't shoot our planes down with surface-to-air missiles. Finally, most missions are accompanied by combat search-and-rescue H-60 helicopters, whose job it is to search for enemy submarines or pick up any aviators unlucky enough to be shot down behind enemy lines. Yet of all the myriad aircraft that make up a tactical attack team, none may be as important to a fighter pilot's well-being as the refueling tankers.

Tankers give fighter jets the ability to refuel in midair, effectively extending their range so they can complete missions far beyond what the jet's fuel reserves would normally allow. This is especially important in light of the fact that an F/A-18's fuel consumption can vary greatly, depending on how the plane is operated. An F/A-18 has a maximum range of about 1,100 nautical miles (1,200 miles), but during combat that can drop to as low as 400 nautical miles (approximately 460 miles). Pilots who constantly have to use the afterburners while dogfighting in close quarters with enemy aircraft can use their entire fuel supply in as little as twenty minutes. The other variable is that plans always change in combat. In my experience, even the most detailed plans can go out the window once the plane is airborne.

When I was flying combat missions in Iraq during Operation Iraqi Freedom, my orders may have called for me to drop ordnance on an enemy cave, only to have weather move in and force a change of targets. Or find out that a squad of soldiers on the ground was being overrun by enemy combatants and needed immediate air support. Or enemy craft had suddenly made aggressive moves toward a US ship five hundred miles away that now needed air support. In situations like that, adaptation is key and teamwork is essential.

One of the most challenging scenarios is when a tanker goes "sour" and can no longer provide fuel, for one reason or another. In these cases, the situation can become *in extremis* quickly, and pilots need to immediately locate and coordinate with another tanker to continue their mission, and maybe even avoid disaster. Failing that, the options become less and less desirable, especially in combat. Take Iraq, for example. With no other options, I could land in Baghdad and hope to find a safe place to park and coordinate getting gas, though setting a US fighter jet down in the heart of enemy territory is never a good idea. Ejecting over open water is another possibility if the mission takes place in blue water, though perhaps even less attractive than the first. In most cases, a fighter pilot will change altitude and speed to conserve gas (though that only buys a limited amount of time), then make plans to connect with another tanker before the situation turns critical.

Given this kind of variability—and the somewhat disconcerting fact that there are no side-of-the-road gas stations to visit and no friendlies on the ground willing to lend me ten thousand extra pounds of jet fuel—fighter pilots are *always* thinking about their fuel state and the location of their tankers. Tankers come in a variety of shapes and sizes. A typical Navy tanker is an F/A-18 Super Hornet with a tank called an ARS (Aerial Refueling Store) attached to the bottom, while the Air Force tends to use much larger KC-10s or KC-135s. These last are massive, passenger-airline-sized crafts, and can hold upward of 200,000 pounds of fuel in specially designed fuselage tanks.

Since both planes are traveling at approximately 300 mph, the process of transferring fuel from a tanker to a fighter jet is a delicate one and demands extensive teamwork between the aircrafts' pilots. First a location and altitude are chosen, one that the tanker reaches a few minutes before the fighter jet. When the jet arrives, it approaches from a mile behind and 1,000 feet below the tanker, then begins to close the gap.

The actual refueling process usually takes one of two forms. With Air Force tankers and fighters, it's more common to use what's called a flying boom system. In that scenario, the Air Force jet maneuvers to a stern position about fifty feet behind the tanker.

Once the two planes are perfectly coordinated in terms of speed and course, the boom operator on the tanker—who is in constant communication with the fighter jet—extends a long tube with small guide wings on the end (the boom) that can insert a connection into a receptacle on the receiving jet. The fuel is transferred at high pressure through the tube, which can be extended and retracted as weather and circumstances dictate. The boom automatically disconnects if the receiving plane moves off track for any reason, such as a sudden change in weather, turbulence, the appearance of enemy aircraft, or some other unexpected turn.

Navy jets can accept gas from either Air Force or Navy tankers, in both cases through what's known as a drogue system. With this system, the tanker extends a seventy-five-foot flexible hose with a soft basket (which looks like a very small parachute) on the end of it. The fighter jet then raises the three-foot-long Inflight Refueling (IFR) probe housed on the right side of the fuselage forward of the cockpit, which clicks into the basket and initiates the fuel transfer. It's up to the fighter pilot to maneuver the jet, in calm air and in turbulence, to make the connection and begin fuel transfer. We do it day and night, in good weather and bad.

I found that aerial refueling could be fairly nerve-racking . . . but not always. On some days the process was peaceful, almost serene: the sun setting, the sky ablaze with orange light, and the two planes moving as if welded together. At other times, the weather wasn't as cooperative and the tanker and basket bounced around like a kid on a trampoline. I've had to refuel in the midst of thunder and lightning storms, trying desperately not to become disoriented as we raced through dense cloud cover.

Once, as a young pilot with my first F/A-18 squadron of

VFA-97, we were performing night operations in blue water conditions in the middle of the Pacific Ocean and I was having a night "in the barrel." We use that term to describe situations where a fighter pilot is having a hard time landing on the carrier and continually goes up and around, over and over again, trying to land, like the barrel of a washing machine. I had boltered a few times, my tailhook either skipping over the wires or my approach too high to catch a wire. My gas was getting low.

That's when I got the call from the approach controllers in charge of all air operations to join with the recovery tanker circling over the ship and get some fuel. Aircraft carriers will almost always have a recovery tanker in the air during training and combat missions, particularly at night or when the weather is bad.

The responsibility of the recovery tanker pilot is to listen to the radio chatter and know the gas states of everybody in the air. This way, if someone's having trouble, tanker pilots can get themselves to the perfect position when needed. It's an important job because the fighter pilot needing gas is likely already stressed out by their inability to land, the weather, and/or their low fuel level, like I was that day.

"Four oh five," the controller transmitted on the common radio frequency said. "Hook up, clean up, signal Tank. Angels 4 tanker button 19, clear to switch." (Translation: Raise your arresting hook, raise your landing gear, join with the tanker aircraft at 4,000 feet overhead the ship to get some gas, and switch your radio to channel 19 to coordinate with the tanker.)

"Four oh five," I replied succinctly. "Copy all, switching." (Translation: I hear you and understand what you want me to do, no matter how easy or hard it might appear to be at the time.)

Already struggling, now I was faced with the challenge of finding and connecting with the tanker in the dark, in the clouds, and in the midst of a storm.

"Tanker, this is 405," I said on the new frequency. "I'm at Angels 4 looking for a drink."

Luckily, the tanker pilot—a fellow senior pilot named Rusty—wasn't stressed at all. In a perfectly calm airline pilot voice that I'll never forget, he smoothly replied, "Hey, 405, I'm right in front of you at your two o'clock. Once we come through this cloud, you'll be clear to join."

Sure enough, as soon as I punched through that massive storm cloud, there was Rusty in the tanker, drogue probe out and waiting for me to connect. He had done his part by monitoring what was happening with me, knew where I was, paid attention to the pattern, knew I was going to need gas (likely before I did), and got himself in the perfect position. All I had to do was flip a single switch on my left-hand side behind the throttles to raise the IFR probe and connect with the tanker's refueling basket to get my much-needed gas.

As my tanks filled and we flew together in sync for the next ten minutes, I breathed a huge sigh of relief. All I wanted to do was hug Rusty, but I still had to land. As I disconnected from the basket, he spoke to me again.

"All right, 405," he said. "You got this. The ship is back to your left at seven o'clock. I'll see you on deck."

It was still night, it was still dark, and it was still scary. But Rusty had given me that little boost of confidence I needed to calm down and land.

I never actually flew as a tanker pilot until I was commanding officer of the *Teddy Roosevelt*. Even as CO, I made a point to fly at least twice a week, but given my position it was impossible for me to do so during active combat missions, when my place was on the bridge of the ship. But whenever I could, I went up in the air and flew as a tanker pilot. Every time I did, I thought about Rusty and the importance of the tanker's role to the team. It wasn't the MVP position I had craved in my early days, but I knew the job was just as crucial nonetheless.

~~~~~~

As critical as its individual parts may be to a team's success, an equally important (yet often overlooked) element of success is how leaders manage the people around them. For me, one of the key aspects of leadership, no matter what the circumstance or scenario, boils down to this: understand the importance of each and every person to the team, make sure they know it, then delegate to them the power to perform to their fullest potential.

The flip side, of course, comes when people are scared of being responsible for things that are out of their control and then fail to successfully delegate to those around them. They refuse to let anyone have control over anything—even the little things— because they are so scared it might go wrong. The product of such a mindset is an organization so incredibly micromanaged that nothing gets done, at least not without prior approval and oversight by "the boss." It makes for a difficult place to work, and a very ineffective organization.

Over the course of my career, I worked for a few people who acted this way. In each case, the department quickly developed a stovepipe mentality where each staff member could only look up through their own personal chimney for approbation from the top, because everything was being micromanaged by one or two people. It's a slow and inefficient way to operate in any business, but particularly in the military. You can't fight wars that way, and I'd argue you can't succeed in the business world that way, either.

As the late general Colin Powell said, delegate to the point where you are uncomfortable. But remember that no matter how much you delegate, the person at the top remains responsible. Accept that truth and everyone around you will thrive. And so will you.

I witnessed this firsthand when I was named CO of the *Theodore Roosevelt* and quickly realized there was no way on earth I was going to be able to account for everything that happened on board. I couldn't be everywhere, and I couldn't do it all.

One of the most significant stepping-stones on my part was handing over the navigation and "driving" of the $10 billion ship. Doing so is not necessarily unusual for the CO of a ship, but every captain has to determine his or her own level of comfort and decide how much they want to delegate. Some spend every possible moment on the bridge overseeing and micromanaging their junior officers, while others are comfortable delegating authority. I always chose the latter option, for two reasons: (1) it allowed the people around me to grow stronger and more confident, and (2) it afforded me the freedom to address the myriad other things on the ship that also required my attention.

That said, I knew that if anything went wrong, I would ultimately be responsible for it, so I had to ensure my team was trained and ready to handle anything that might come up. This was particularly challenging when we were steaming through the crowded waters of the South China Sea, which are peppered with thousands of vessels of every shape and size, each one of which presents a potential risk of accidental contact.

It's not like a collision would have done much damage to the carrier. There are few things on the ocean that can put a dent in a US Navy aircraft carrier. To the contrary, the *Roosevelt* would have destroyed just about anything it came in contact with. And in a part of the world where thousands of people feed their families by fishing in small wooden boats, the risk of contact was significant . . . and perilous. Fishing nets would be torn to shreds, boats destroyed, civilians killed.

Add to this the thousands of cargo ships that ply the world's waters every day, and you can see why handing over control of the ship is not something you do lightly. South of Malaysia, the Strait of Malacca—a narrow stretch of water some 580 miles long—represents the main shipping channel between the Indian and Pacific Oceans, and one of the most important shipping lanes in the world. It's also one of the most congested. Approximately half of all the world's oceanborne goods travel through those waters, massive tankers and cargo vessels weaving their way among humble fishing boats with nothing more than a lantern to indicate their presence.

Collide with any of those larger vessels and people can die, for which the CO of the ship will ultimately be responsible, and likely relieved of duty. It's a high-stakes proposition, but one all commanding officers accept.

Even though we may have been entering a freeway of vessels all simultaneously navigating a narrow body of water like the Strait of Malacca, the simple truth was that I couldn't always be on the bridge. I may have been the Sailor with the most well-trained eye, but I wasn't the *only* person capable of navigating the ship, and I also had to sleep, eat, and take care of the countless other things happening on any given day. So I had to trust that my senior navigator and the ship's junior officers and their bridge teams would navigate the *Roosevelt* safely, even when I couldn't be there to guide them.

Once again, I drew comfort from the bridge team's training and expertise. To become an officer of the deck, a junior officer has to successfully complete a rigorous and extensive training regimen culminating with a board exam that sees the candidate grilled by a panel of the ship's senior officers regarding navigation and the "rules of the road" (maritime traffic laws) in a variety of stressful situations. So it didn't matter to me that many of these junior officers had only been in the Navy for a couple of years. To qualify as an officer of the deck is a huge achievement, and demonstrates a level of leadership and expertise that few folks ever possess.

While I trusted these intelligent, competent, and well-trained officers to handle their bridge teams and the *Roosevelt* under any circumstance, it was never lost on me that any problems or issues we ran into—figuratively or literally—were ultimately *my* responsibility. I accepted that fact, perhaps even embraced it. I delegated until it hurt and we trusted each other to do the right thing. Bolstered by that knowledge and strong in my convictions, I owned the responsibility that came along with my leadership, in good times and bad.

You can have the strongest people at your command, but they will never perform to the best of their abilities if you hold the reins too tight. Give them the tools to run freely and I guarantee they're going to produce more, just like Senior Chief Foresman's Clydesdales.

It's taken me a while to realize, but now I see it. The math works after all.

CHAPTER 6

Play Small Ball

As a kid growing up in California, baseball was a big deal. We listened to it, we watched it, we talked about it, and we played it. A lot. I settled in at third base, a position that suited my size, speed, and reasonable hand-eye coordination. And while I never got good enough to play for my beloved San Francisco Giants, I did play in the Rincon Valley Little League Majors, which was the next-best thing for a young kid at the time. The best team I ever played on as a kid was the Dragons, led by our larger-than-life Coach Ray, who proved to be a memorable figure in my life, even though I was just a boy of twelve when I met him.

A huge man who also happened to be a California Highway Patrol officer, Coach Ray was a stickler for the fundamentals. Under his guidance, I and all the other kids on the team mastered the foundational elements of the game, which we carried with us throughout our little league "careers." I remember him hitting grounder after grounder after grounder to me at third base, a seemingly endless barrage of balls hit in my general direction, all with a singular collective purpose: to reinforce the importance of learning how to do the little things right. I didn't know it at the time, but Coach Ray was teaching me the value of what baseball aficionados call *small ball*.

In small ball, a team relies on the fundamentals to win games. On the offensive side, singles and walks are as valuable as extra-base hits, and advancing runners through steals, bunts, hit-and-runs, and sacrifices is every bit as important as waiting for the long ball to clear the bases. In the field, teams that play small ball are defensive masters, and rarely give their opponents the gift of free runs.

Although small ball was once the dominant style of play across the major leagues, its popularity has waned dramatically in recent decades with the advent of smaller ballparks and the ever-increasing lust for home runs by both teams and their fans. Nevertheless, there are occasional examples of clubs employing the small-ball strategy to beat the odds and humble their opponents. In the 1950s, the Chicago White Sox had very few power hitters, so manager Paul Richards decided to manufacture runs through a combined emphasis on speed and defense, and a rigorous adherence to the basics. The so-called Go-Go Sox were born and went on to win the American League championship in 1959. The Los Angeles Dodgers won two World Series titles in the 1960s the same way.

More recently, the Kansas City Royals—a team regarded by most pundits as a playoff long shot—out-bunted, out-stole, and out-fundamentaled their opponents all the way to a World Series appearance in 2014, where they ultimately lost to my Giants, four games to three. The loss did little to dampen the spirits of the resolute Royals. Under manager Ned Yost, the team entered the 2015 season again as long shots (oddsmakers gave them an approximately 2 percent chance of winning the World Series), then did exactly what they had done the year before. Focusing on those same fundamentals that had brought his team so far in 2014, Yost led the Royals to a World Series victory in 2015, defeating the New York Mets four games to one.

Surprisingly, the same approach can be found in the Navy. In a military setting, training is as elemental as breathing. Your training dictates how efficiently your ship runs, how well your crew responds in critical situations, and how effectively you can face adversity. As an aircraft carrier pilot, small ball meant practicing our landings hundreds of times before we progressed to actually doing them on the deck of an aircraft carrier. We started in the simulator, then eventually graduated to actual runways, where every landing was critiqued and graded. Only after we had expertly demonstrated our proficiency in the fundamentals were we allowed to graduate to the real deal and land on an aircraft carrier at sea. Even then, we were assessed every time we touched down. I may have risen to become the commanding officer of the USS *Theodore Roosevelt* many years later, but every single time I flew in an F/A-18, my landings on the carrier were scrutinized for how well I performed the fundamentals of that basic yet unforgiving task.

I've tried to take the value of small ball to heart in everything I've done, both in and out of the military. In combat, you cannot afford to lose. In the civilian world, the consequences may not be as dire, but the message is the same. Master the fundamentals, and you'll find it much easier to navigate the path to success. Because in the end, we practice *not* until we get it right, but so we never get it wrong.

~~~~~

One of the benefits of extensive training is that at a certain point the things we do become instinctive, almost reflexive. By becoming so well versed in the fundamental components of your craft, whatever that may be, you can move on to the higher-level thinking demanded by more complex tasks. Adaptability, it would seem, is one of the best by-products of fundamental proficiency. Never was that made more apparent to me than on one of the worst days in American history, September 11, 2001.

On that fateful morning, nineteen militants affiliated with the Islamic extremist group Al Qaeda hijacked four passenger jets and carried out suicide attacks against targets in the US. The most devastating of these were the two planes that slammed into the World Trade Center in New York City, a cowardly act that resulted in the deaths of almost three thousand innocent people.

At that time, I had recently made the transition from helicopter to fighter pilot and was a relatively new F/A-18 student in Lemoore, California. I had an early training flight that day and would be making my first live bombing runs in one of our ranges in the Nevada desert. But as I pulled into the base and heard news of the first jet hitting the towers, my gut told me that the day—and the world—had just changed dramatically.

As the media began to sift through the news of the crash and determine whether or not it was an accident, my instructor, two other students, and I settled into the briefing room to prepare for the mission ahead. Then we got the news that the second tower had also been struck by a passenger jet. For the first time that morning, we understood that the first plane was not just an accident and that a concerted effort was under way to attack America.

In seconds, the talk in the briefing room of our upcoming training hop evaporated. There was no way we were going to fly around the Nevada desert while the rest of the country tried to deal with the tragedy that was quickly unfolding in New York. More importantly, there was a chance that similar terrorist attacks were planned in other parts of the country, including California. As airports and military bases across the United States were systematically shut down, we realized that we were among the few qualified fighter pilots on a military base in the state that had pilots, jets, and weapons available. Quickly our conversation turned: How were we going to defend California's many landmarks should the same situation soon present itself in our backyard?

Before long, the commanding officer, or "skipper," of the squadron entered the briefing room.

"Ladies and gentlemen," he said. "Hornet's Nest; three minutes sharp."

The Hornet's Nest is the primary briefing room in Lemoore. Named after the F/A-18 Hornets we fly, it has several rows of tiered seating surrounding a primary presentation area. We gathered the few pilots who were on the base at that early hour and listened attentively as the skipper addressed us.

"Folks, I have just received a call from the air boss [the admiral in charge of all US naval aviation] down in San Diego, and at this time they don't know much more than we do," he said. "But it would seem that an attack on the West Coast, and particularly California, is possible.

"As you know, the responsibility of defending the California airspace in these circumstances would typically fall to the Fresno Air National Guard," he continued. "But the FAA has shut down all airspace, so most of the reservists that fly out of Fresno can't even get there to man their jets.

"And so, folks," he said, looking at us severely, "that responsibility has fallen to us. We've got the airplanes, we've got the pilots, and we've got some weapons. So we need to figure out how we're going to protect the state should it come to that."

What followed was a discussion the likes of which none of us had experienced before. For as much as the Navy believes in training for any eventuality, nobody in that room had ever considered the possibility of a passenger airline being used as a weapon of mass destruction, let alone how an F/A-18 might take that jet down, if that's what it came to.

With no specific training to fall upon, we began to use our knowledge of the fundamentals of aircraft, aviation, and human nature to tackle a number of different possible scenarios. We decided that should an attack be headed toward California, the terrorists would likely seek to destroy an emotional monument, such as the Golden Gate Bridge or even the symbolic Hollywood area of Los Angeles.

Once we had finalized a list of potential targets—which included skyscrapers, densely populated areas, and key symbolic structures like the Golden Gate Bridge—we needed to decide how to deploy the limited resources we had available. We divided the aircraft and pilots in the squadron into four sections, where each section was a grouping of two jets. One section would be airborne at all times to monitor potential landmarks while simultaneously looking out for inbound airliners. The second section would be on alert, ready to launch at the first notification of suspicious activity, while the third and fourth would be on standby. As we became aware of the additional attacks on the Pentagon and the possible failed attack on the US Capitol, we knew time was of the essence and we needed to get fighters airborne immediately.

Finally, our discussion turned to what would be the most important—and yet most troubling—part of our theoretical duties: taking down an airliner full of passengers to prevent it from destroying even more lives and property. Ethical considerations aside (and we did not have the luxury of time to engage in ethical discussions), we turned our attention to the practical: how does a relatively small, 40,000-pound F/A-18 take down a fully loaded passenger jet weighing as much as 200,000 pounds?

I imagine most people think this would not even be an issue at all. I mean, we're flying *fighter jets*, for goodness' sake. Shouldn't it be child's play to take down a big, lumbering passenger plane flown by relatively untrained pilots? The answer, we realized, was no.

First, we'd have to intercept the passenger jet, which meant figuring out where it was coming from, getting radar on it, then maneuvering the F/A-18 into attack position. That part was challenging enough, based on the sheer size of California. Once we had located the plane, though, the next step would be to stop it, likely by shooting it out of the sky, not necessarily an easy task in light of the fact that most of the weapons we might otherwise have loaded up with were on our ships at the time, not on the base.

There were a few AIM-9 Sidewinder heat-seeking missiles in Lemoore, in anticipation of an upcoming training exercise. Those would be our best chance at success, but if they didn't manage to take the plane down, our only hope would be to pump enough 20mm bullets into the jet to cause catastrophic failure to an engine, wing, or (preferably) both.

We knew a hijacked jet wouldn't just sit there and allow this to happen, though. Being accurate with a nose-mounted machine gun is difficult enough under ideal conditions. Throw in the turbulence caused by a plane of that size and the unpredictability of a pilot hell-bent on terror and destruction, and we soon realized that our chances of taking the plane out by conventional means were slim.

The mood in the Hornet's Nest turned reflective, almost somber. I was still a very rookie fighter pilot, but for those in the room experienced enough to know what needed to be done, there were very few viable options. Then the skipper voiced what the rest of us had feared, but could not say.

"This is an unforgiving task," he said, "but it is our charge nonetheless. If you get to the point where you have to shoot down a hijacked airplane, start with whatever missile you might be carrying. From there switch to your twenty-millimeter gun. And if that doesn't work, your only option is to fly your plane directly into the attacking jet. And in that case, the cockpit is the preferred target."

Thankfully, it never came to that. The tragic events of that day were limited to the East Coast and we never had to test our theories about using F/A-18s to intercept passenger jets. Nevertheless, it would be a few days before the members of the Air National Guard were able to get to their bases and man their planes. So in the interim, those few pilots who were on hand in Lemoore took up the torch.

In the end, the processes we went through on September 11 reflected much of military life: we prepare for life-threatening events that may or may not happen, but usually don't. That's a good thing, but certainly not something we ever count on. Instead we train for every possibility, master the fundamentals of our profession, and employ those skills wherever and whenever they're needed . . . even if it means sacrificing ourselves for the good of the country.

Although the September 11 attacks were a horrific anomaly, playing small ball means mastering the fundamentals of your craft to the point where you are prepared for almost any event, no matter how rare or unlikely it may be. In the Navy, one such event is the threat of attack by an enemy. From bombs to missiles, submarines to fighter jets, there are a number of ways an enemy could strike at the heart of a US Navy ship, which means damage control is an essential part of our training.

On the USS *Theodore Roosevelt*, we insisted on performing damage control exercises at least once a week, sometimes twice. It was a heavy schedule given the time and energy required, but the way I saw it, few efforts were as important to the overall well-being of the ship. Each exercise simulated a different type of attack, though they all shared a common thread: significant physical damage to the ship and loss of life.

At the beginning of each exercise, our training officer would make what we call a "Training Scenario Report," an announcement over the ship's 1MC intercom system, which ensured that every Sailor on board was aware of what was about to happen. This was followed by a scripted story line read by our intelligence specialists offering background on the situation and preparing the Sailors for what was about to occur.

"The USS *Theodore Roosevelt* is approximately thirty miles off the coast of Country Orange, which is currently experiencing hostilities with Country Purple over a territorial dispute," the intelligence specialist would read. "The US has intervened on behalf of its ally, Country Purple, in an attempt to diffuse the situation, but Country Orange has threatened to attack US ships if they get too close to their coast.

"In addition," he continued, "Country Orange has previously attacked commercial ships and threatened to attack anyone that supports Country Purple. All diplomatic attempts to end hostilities have stalled, and forces in the area remain on high alert."

After a pause of two to three minutes, this was followed by another scenario update, this one far more urgent: "Inbound enemy antiship missiles have been detected from the direction of Country Orange, all hands set General Quarters!" Also known as Battle Stations, General Quarters is a signal for all hands (everyone available) on board a ship to stop what they're doing and immediately man their battle stations.

On a US Navy ship, a call to General Quarters is a big deal, and indicates the highest level of attentiveness and readiness.

Each Sailor knows his or her responsibilities during these scenarios, and leaps into action. In an instant, the ship becomes a hive of activity and urgency. Some Sailors man the guns and defensive missile systems; others prepare to deal with fire and flooding that may occur as a result of an attack. Throughout all of it, medical personnel man battle dressing stations strategically located throughout the ship.

Meanwhile, the damage control officer continued the narrative over the 1MC.

"Missiles inbound, port side, all hands brace for shock," followed by a series of loud explosions played over the 1MC to simulate a missile hit. "We've taken a direct hit on the port side of the ship. There are multiple reports of smoke and fire on the O-3 level port side below the flight deck. Repair Lockers 2 and 7 respond!"

A big part of that response was fire control. Fire in any environment is bad, but on a massive, nuclear-powered aircraft carrier at sea loaded with fuel and bombs, it can be catastrophic if not quickly contained. Within minutes, dozens of Sailors would gather at any number of the ship's repair lockers that are peppered throughout the ship. These centralized areas contain hoses and other firefighting gear, and allow us to attack a fire that could break out anywhere on board, much as a large town will likely have multiple fire stations to provide quick response to emergencies in various locations when required.

While we never set real fires during these exercises, they are intense nonetheless, and often last several hours. Sailors are fully suited in complete firefighting gear, with helmets, masks, and a self-contained breathing apparatus. It's dark and it's hot, and people are yelling at each other as they pull fully pressurized hoses through the narrow steel hallways of the ship in search of the fire. It's grueling, stressful, and exhausting work. So much so, in fact, that from time to time Sailors actually pass out from the effort. To some it may have seemed like overkill, but I knew that when it came to training, there was no such thing.

In fact, my goal was to make the simulation as realistic as possible, so we went as far as to employ smoke machines at various locations throughout the *Roosevelt*. There was no holding back. If we had ten smoke machines on board, then we used every single one. It made for a lot of extra work and a heck of a mess, but I knew it was worth it. Keeping the ship functional and battle-ready while under attack was a fundamental part of our responsibilities, and we were going to make sure every person on board was an expert at it.

The exercises also gave our newest shipmates the opportunity to hone their skills almost immediately upon their arrival on board. By performing training exercises with exhausting regularity, we ensured that everybody was ready to go should the situation arise, from the junior Sailor who just reported from boot camp to the most senior officer on board.

Those situations do indeed arise, sometimes out of the blue and with tragic consequences. In May 1987, the Navy frigate USS *Stark* was attacked with missiles fired from an Iraqi aircraft as the ship patrolled off the Saudi Arabian coast. A total of 37 Sailors were killed in the attack and another 21 injured. Thirteen years later, 17 Sailors on board the USS *Cole* were killed when a group of Al Qaeda terrorists carried out a suicide bombing of the ship while she was refueling in Yemen's Aden Harbor. Another 37 were injured.

Nobody saw either of these attacks coming, but the crews of the *Stark* and the *Cole* had been trained well, and the diligence of those crews kept both ships from suffering more casualties and likely sinking. Damage control takes teamwork, it takes integrity, it takes commitment, and it demands hard work. When push came to shove, I wanted my Sailors to be ready. And they were.

As executive officer of the USS *Ronald Reagan* in 2015, one of my responsibilities was to serve as the ship's senior damage control officer. There were other Sailors whose job it was to attend to the day-to-day nuances of damage control, but I was charged with overseeing all the damage control and training on the ship.

We were sailing the *Reagan* from San Diego to Japan, where we were taking the place of the USS *George Washington* aircraft carrier, which had been stationed there for almost ten years. As part of that change and to show our respect for our Japanese hosts, the *Reagan* was going to participate in what we call a pass-in-review exercise. In this exercise, the *Reagan* would fall in line with a dozen or so other US Navy ships, along with twenty ships from the Japanese navy. It was a symbolic exercise—almost like a parade at sea—to demonstrate the friendship, alliance, and shared values between our two nations, which had once been such bitter enemies.

For us on the *Reagan*, the highlight of the exercise would be a visit from then Japanese prime minister Shinzo Abe, who would go on to become the longest-serving prime minister in the country's history. After arriving on the *Reagan* by helicopter from one of the Japanese ships, the prime minister would be escorted to Captain Bolt's in-port cabin, a formal setting where the ship's captain typically hosts foreign dignitaries while at sea.

I was in my blues, my formal Navy uniform reserved for events of the highest order, making final preparations for the prime minister's impending arrival while Bolter was up on the bridge overseeing the navigation of the ship during the pass-in-review. That's when the brass bells sounded over the 1MC, signaling to the entire ship that something serious had just occurred.

Had it been a training scenario, the sound of the bells (to this day I get jumpy when I hear bells ringing) would have been accompanied by someone calling out, "This is a drill; this is a drill." While I suspected that's what it was (and admonished myself for scheduling a drill so close to the prime minister's arrival), I quickly realized that no such words had been called. Moments later, it became clear what was happening.

"Fire! Fire! Fire!" a voice cried over the 1MC, echoing through the halls of the ship. "Fire, Hangar Bay 1, starboard side!"

Damn.

Although I was hoping it was nothing more than a small trash fire and the person on the 1MC was being overzealous, I bounded down the ladder (stairs) to the hangar bay, where the Air Department damage control experts in charge of the hangar bay were already closing off the thirty-foot-high blast doors that divide the carrier's hangar into three parts. This was no drill: Hangar Bay 1 was already starting to fill with thick smoke.

The source of the smoke was an E-2C Hawkeye aircraft, a highly sophisticated electronics and radar plane used to track the movements of enemy craft. The E-2C was tucked into the forward right corner of Hangar Bay 1 for scheduled maintenance; a thick 450-amp cord connected to the plane was sparking malevolently and smoke billowed from inside the craft. It was a volatile situation; the E-2C was full of fuel and there were other planes in the hangar bay as well.

Moments later the Fire Team arrived on scene, which gave me a second to breathe, collect my thoughts, and call Captain Bolt. As always, Bolter trusted me to handle the situation and did not micromanage. Given that we were still in the midst of our pass-in-review with approximately thirty other ships, his efforts were much better focused on driving the ship and keeping us out of harm's way.

The Fire Team cut the power to the 450-amp cable, but the sparking and smoke continued. Led by our sharpest lead Air Department officer, Lieutenant Kenyato Mayes, they went inside the E-2C only to emerge moments later with troubling news: the sparking had begun to turn to flame, and they were concerned that it might spread to the residual fuel on board the aircraft.

"What do you recommend we do?" I asked.

"Well, sir," Mayes answered, "it doesn't seem we have any other choice but to use the AFFF [aqueous film-forming foam] to put it out."

I knew that using the AFFF, which is extremely acidic, would cause significant damage to the $80 million airplane, but the situation was becoming more urgent with each passing second. The hangar bay was now filled with dark gray, acrid smoke, and we couldn't afford to linger anymore. If we didn't sacrifice the E-2C and the fire spread, things could quickly turn disastrous.

"I trust you to do what needs to be done."

The Fire Team handled the situation efficiently and expertly. They moved with a purpose and synchrony that was inspiring to see, a testament to their extensive and ongoing training. Not long after, the fire was out. A mountain of soapy foam spilled out of the E2 and across the floor of the hangar bay. Still dressed in my formal blues in anticipation of Prime Minister Abe's impending visit, I walked around the plane to make sure there was no lingering risk. Convinced the fire was out, I updated Bolter on the situation, then hustled up to the flight deck to greet the prime minister and escort him to the in-port cabin. I also had our public affairs officer communicate with the prime minister's staff that we had had a fire on board the *Reagan* but all was now safe.

Shortly after the prime minister's helicopter touched down, we faced each other shaking hands and warmly greeting one another. As we all stood there chatting, I couldn't help but notice that he kept looking down at my feet. At first I thought this may have been a simple cultural difference between our two nations, but I soon realized what had drawn his attention. I still had a noticeable lather of soapy foam over much of my black leather dress shoes.

I was slightly embarrassed, but the prime minister just smiled and gave me a wink.

I smiled back. "Never a dull day at sea, sir," I said.

~~~~~

Small-ball mastery of the fundamentals will eventually get you to the point where your actions require almost no thinking. Another product of such expertise is the ability to quickly recognize when things are out of the ordinary and you need to deviate from your reflexive actions. This wasn't always evident to me. As a military man, I generally trusted my training and the orders I received. So if a course of action was ordered, I followed it. Unless I realized those actions might actually kill innocent civilians, that is.

In March 2003, the United States embarked upon Operation Iraqi Freedom, a military action initiated by President George W. Bush when the Iraqi government was suspected to be importing and stockpiling weapons of mass destruction. For me it represented my first combat deployment as an F/A-18 fighter pilot.

On the day in question, I launched from the USS *Nimitz* aircraft carrier at first light as the junior pilot in a two-aircraft section. Our mission that morning was to patrol an area north of Baghdad in search of a battalion of tanks that the Iraqis had apparently hidden in some palm forests there. We were flying relatively low over the area in search of the tanks when suddenly my plane's radar warning receiver (RWR) started screaming at me: I had been targeted by an SA-2 surface-to-air missile (SAM).

Although this was the first time I had ever been targeted by an enemy in a live combat mission, I didn't panic. I fell back onto my training and began to work through the procedures that had been drilled into my head so many times that they had become automatic.

I let my wingman know what was going on as I scanned the horizon for the inbound missile, but didn't see the telltale smokey trail of a missile the size of a telephone pole racing in my direction. It was a clear day and I could see for miles, but I didn't trust my senses completely; the missile could still be coming from any direction. More importantly, my jet was still warning me of an imminent strike. Inside my helmet it was impossible to ignore the distinctive, high-pitched warble that indicates an incoming missile attack; the jet's HUD (head-up display) continued to indicate that I had been targeted.

I began to instinctively fly the F/A-18 aggressively in a series of planned maneuvers, rolling from one side to the other to get eyes on the incoming SA-2. Once I saw it (and assuming it was still tracking my jet), I was hoping to take last-ditch evasive action to avoid it blowing me out of the sky. A surface-to-air missile can travel at incredible speeds (as fast as 2,000 mph), but that speed and its small wings are also its Achilles' heel. In an F/A-18, you can easily make a full 180-degree turn in less than two or three miles. An SA-2, on the other hand, is an older technology and needs between five and ten miles to make the same turn. So if I saw it coming, the theory was that I could turn more quickly than it could, causing it to overshoot me. By then, the hope was that it wouldn't have enough energy to make it back to me, since surface-to-air missiles have a finite range. (Things are different today, since most surface-to-air missiles are far more maneuverable and armed with improved proximity fuses that can detect when they're close to a target and detonate without the need for a direct hit.)

Still, I saw nothing, and neither did my wingman.

My heart was racing, my breaths inside my oxygen mask were short and tight, adrenaline raced through my veins. Although I was completely focused on the mission and had no time to think about anything other than the life-or-death situation I was in, I was happy I had followed standard procedure before the mission and written farewell letters to Mary, Connor, and Sean (Mary was pregnant with our son Ian at the time) before I left.

My plane was fully loaded with fuel, bombs, and extra tanks of gas. It was near its maximum weight, and therefore wasn't nearly as nimble as it otherwise may have been. With each maneuver I performed to get eyes on the missile, I bled off a bit of airspeed and lost altitude. I used the afterburners to try to keep my speed up, but that began to use up a fair bit of my fuel reserves. My wingman had quickly taken up a position at a higher altitude in an attempt to find the missile and possibly talk my eyes on it should he have spotted it first.

As a result of all my maneuvering to try to find the missile, I fell to the lowest altitude and airspeed preferred for combat over hostile territory, which made me extremely vulnerable to subsequent attacks. I needed to quickly regain both to make sure my first combat tour would not be my last. My training dictated my next step: "slick off the jet," which meant performing an emergency jettison of everything extraneous on board, namely all my bombs and extra tanks of highly volatile jet fuel.

The bombs would leave the plane inert, and therefore wouldn't detonate upon impact with the ground. But they were still exceptionally large and heavy (each weighed over a thousand pounds), and when dropped from approximately 10,000 feet would do extraordinary damage to whatever they hit on the ground beneath me. The potential for civilian casualties was high.

Yet the plane continued to chirp at me, warning me that the missile was inbound. Only a matter of seconds had elapsed, but it felt like a lifetime, a lifetime that could theoretically be coming to an abrupt end. And yet I found it difficult to punch off the extra weight just to lighten my load. Sure, I didn't want to get hit. But I also couldn't live with the greater potential of killing innocent people on the ground, either. Plus, my wingman hadn't seen the inbound missile, and something just didn't *feel* right.

My HUD was still lit up like a Christmas tree with warnings of the missile, but I had never managed to put eyes on it. By now at least thirty seconds had elapsed, and if it was going to reach me, it should have done so by now. So I decided to wait on the decision to slick off the jet, even if it meant I would remain more vulnerable to an inbound missile.

No sooner had I made my decision that the warnings disappeared. Just like that. One second I was about to meet my maker, and the next all was quiet in the jet once again. I inhaled slowly and deliberately in an attempt to slow my heart rate, then scanned the horizon for any last sign of the missile.

Nothing.

Having used up a good part of my fuel supply during my maneuvers, my wingman and I met up with a nearby tanker to refuel, then turned back toward the *Nimitz*. It was a one-hour flight back to the ship, and I needed every minute for my heart rate to come back down to normal.

In the debrief room following the flight, I told my squadron mates the story of having been targeted by the mysterious disappearing missile.

"That's the third or fourth report we've gotten of the same phenomenon," said Ensign Smith, one of the ship's intelligence officers, as nonchalantly as if he were reporting the weather. "We're not one hundred percent sure what's going on but it seems as though when the Air Force's F-15s lock us up on their radars, the software inadvertently triggers the signal in the jet that you're being targeted with a SAM."

Well. That would have been good to know, say, six or seven hours ago. Yet as frustrated as I may have been with learning this information *after* I had returned from one of the more "exciting" flights I'd had in a few years, I managed to breathe a sigh of relief nonetheless.

I was still a relatively new fighter pilot, and it was my first experience being targeted during live combat. But because I had trained so extensively on the ground and had mastered the small-ball fundamentals of my craft, I knew something wasn't quite right. Call it intuition if you will, but I think it was more likely the product of my training. As a result, I instinctively knew how unlikely it would have been for me to be targeted for that long without me or my wingman spotting the missile *somewhere*. And when we didn't, it was that same small-ball training that had allowed me to make the correct split-second decision to *not* jettison my bombs and drop tanks. It was a decision that had likely saved the lives of innocent people.

~~~~~

I spent the first six months of 2005 deployed to the Persian Gulf with the carrier *Nimitz* as part of VFA-94. Although our responsibilities as part of that F/A-18 squadron were many and varied, one of our primary tasks was to operate over Iraq, with whom the US had had an extremely tense relationship since the US-led invasion of that country in March 2003. While things had settled down considerably by 2005, we still had ground forces operating in various capacities in the country, providing security, hunting for terrorists, and rebuilding the country's infrastructure. Air support was a vital part of those operations, and especially important given the increasing risk of possibility for random acts of violence from rogue elements against US and coalition forces.

On one such mission, I was flying as part of a two-plane section with my wingman Mocha, an outstanding junior pilot who had impressed me since the day she joined the squadron.

Mocha and I had launched off the *Nimitz* and were scheduled to fly north across the Persian Gulf, beyond Baghdad to the area near the Iraqi–Syrian border. It was a long trip, and one that would require us to meet up with tankers for midair refueling several times along the way.

All things considered, it seemed like a relatively benign day. There had been some hostile activity in the area overnight, but tempers seemed to have cooled with morning. Nevertheless, we knew that the possibility of having to target enemies was always a possibility, hence our planes were fully loaded with a complement of 500-pound GBU-12 LGBs (laser-guided bombs) and GBU-38s (GPS-guided bombs), as well as several hundred 20mm rounds for our M61A1 Gatling guns.

As Mocha and I made our way northward, we received word that a squad of Marines that was providing security in the area was pinned down by rogue fighters firing at them from the rooftops in the city of Haditha, some 160 miles northwest of Baghdad. At the same time, the residents of the city had begun to protest against the fact that they had lost access to basic services like water, sewage, and electricity. A large group of these people had amassed angrily near the center of the city, not far from the Marines.

"Roger that, Snake," I replied. "We've got about twenty minutes of play time [based on our fuel levels] and are carrying two by GBU-12, two by GBU-38, and about seven hundred rounds of twenty-millimeter. Have you guys engaged the hostiles yet?"

"Negative," he replied. "But the potshots are escalating, and we are worried that we're going to have to engage soon if we want to leave here."

"We'll be there in three minutes," I told him.

Although we hadn't yet been cleared to drop ordnance on the enemy positions, both Mocha and I knew that the risk for collateral damage was too high. The civilian protestors were so close to the area in question that even the slightest error in the location of our bombs would have killed dozens of innocent people. It was a bad situation.

Ninety seconds later, Mocha and I arrived overhead Haditha. To the east of the city's main road, the enemy combatants had positioned themselves on the rooftops of the surrounding buildings and were taking occasional shots at the Marines, who were holed up in a building on the west side of the street. In the middle were the civilians, innocent people who were frustrated and simply wanted to have their lives return to some semblance of normalcy. The Marines were more than capable of firing back, but based on the growing excitement of the crowd, they wisely realized that any action on their part would likely escalate the chaos . . . and the risk to civilians on the street.

My radio chirped again.

"Dagger One," Snake 01 said. "We are quickly running out of options. We don't want to engage the enemy because we feel it's going to make the situation worse and increase the risk of collateral damage. But once the enemy dials in on our position and starts targeting us with something heavier [like mortars], we're going to have no choice but to engage."

That's when we decided to play small ball.

"Snake," I said, "how about a 'show of force' with a low flyby and a couple of flares to scare away the protestors and either scare away the enemy, or at least provide some cover so you guys can maneuver to the west?"

"Roger that, Dagger," Snake replied. The flares—used by combat pilots for aircraft defense against incoming heat-seeking surface-to-air missiles—posed no risk of fire to surrounding structures, since they are very small and dissipate rapidly. But they are extremely bright and emit a pretty frightening hissing noise when released. That—combined with the sheer force of an F/A-18 roaring by at top speed—might just be enough to create a large enough lull in the action for the Marines to maneuver to a better position.

Over the next few seconds, Mocha and I finalized our plan of attack. I would go in first for a low pass a couple hundred feet off the ground, shooting off my flares just as I crossed above the position in question. Mocha would provide high cover and keep an eye on things, then we'd swap positions and she would come in and do the same some fifteen seconds behind me. It was far less than our jets were capable of, but we knew this "show of force" was our only chance at ensuring the well-being of the Marines while also protecting the civilians.

We circled the city and came in for our runs, all the while chatting with the Marines on the ground. Of course, coming in so close to the ground (and enemy combatants) vastly increased the risk of us being targeted with a surface-to-air missile, but we were confident that the Marines had enough eyes on the enemy to let us know if that was about to happen. Luckily, we'd be going too fast to be hit with a shoulder-fired RPG (rocket-propelled grenade).

I blew in first at 500 knots (approximately 575 mph), the sound of my F/A-18's twin engines exploding off the rooftops of the city just below me. As I looked out from the cockpit, people began to scatter in all directions, their pace becoming furious once I shot off my flares. Then I pulled up, swung around to the south, and watched Mocha do the same. By the time she finished her pass, nobody—enemy included—was left in the vicinity of the Marines, who were able to extract themselves by safely getting to their vehicles and moving to the hills to the west of the city.

Moments later, the Marines hailed us on the radio once again.

"Dagger Flight, that was awesome!" Snake said. "Great air show. Everybody's running for cover, and we're maneuvering safely to the west. We appreciate the help and owe you a beer the next time we see you."

"Roger that, Snake," I replied. "Glad we could help, and we'll certainly take you up on that beer if we see you in port."

For a junior pilot like Mocha, the exchange was one of the more exciting missions of her young career and demonstrated how important it was for us to be flexible in combat situations. One minute you might be flying a routine overwatch security mission and the next you're making yourself a prime target for a surface-to-air missile. For me, it was one of the most satisfying missions I'd ever been on, because we managed to protect our troops on the ground and didn't have to destroy anything or kill anybody to do it.

As combat pilots, we're trained to drop ordnance on enemies when the situation demands it. That's the biggest hammer we carry in our toolbox. But in this case, the hammer was rendered useless, and we were forced to look at all our other tools as well. It wasn't blowing up the Death Star; it wasn't a grand slam in the bottom of the ninth. It was a simple maneuver that we had to execute precisely to be successful. And because we had mastered the fundamentals of our game, that's exactly what we did.

By our nature, pilots have a way of focusing on the details. Our pre- and post-flight briefings are long, usually several hours longer than the flights themselves, and many of our training missions are flown simply to practice basic skills like formation flying or aircraft carrier landings. But at the same time, we know that the more time we spend hammering out the nuances of our missions and the more time we practice the basics, the more successful the flight will be for everyone involved. Then, when the time comes for us to execute our skill under the most stressful circumstances in the real world, we'll be ready.

So while on the inside you may just be a twelve-year-old kid who's tired of fielding grounder after grounder after grounder, there's no arguing with the results. Small ball actually does win games.

CHAPTER 7

Surf When You Can

In early 1779, British explorer and naval captain James Cook found himself amid the Hawaiian Islands as part of a four-year voyage of the British Royal Navy's HMS *Resolution*. During one particular pass of the Oahu coastline, Cook noticed a number of young locals participating in an activity neither he nor any of his crew had ever witnessed. The kids were lying in the water on long, narrow wooden boards, patiently awaiting the break of a wave, at which point they would turn to shore, paddle madly, then hop up and ride the board shoreward.

"The motion is so rapid for near the space of a stone's throw," Cook wrote in his log, "that they seem to fly on the water, the flight of a bird being hardly quicker than theirs."

I'm no Captain Cook (thank goodness; they say Cook was later killed, disemboweled, and roasted), but I too needed Hawaii to open my eyes to the joys of surfing. It's not like I hadn't been introduced to the sport before. As a California kid, I'd surfed a few times in my youth, but never lived close enough to the ocean to make it a habit, so it never stuck. But in Hawaii, surfing was life and life was surfing.

So when I arrived at Barbers Point in 1995 to join my helicopter squadron, I knew that surfing was bound to become an important part of my routine. I was young, Mary and I had no children, and my professional responsibilities were relatively light outside of flying. If I ever wanted to learn how to surf, this was the time.

Enter Russ "Rusty" Keaulana. A professional surfer and local legend, Russ was the namesake of Keaulana's, a western Oahu surf shop I'd heard about through a friend of a friend. After a dinner out one night, Mary and I gathered the courage to venture to one of Keaulana's shops in search of a board, where I soon settled on a nine-foot Russ-K. Maneuverable without being twitchy, yet long enough to handle a heavy-footed rookie, the Russ-K turned out to be the perfect board for me.

Although I didn't realize it at the time, the board wasn't just my vehicle to surf waves. I was also being given the gift of "living *pono*," the Hawaiian value of living a balanced life with righteousness and care for those around you. The next day, my love affair with surfing began.

Desperate to master the craft as quickly as possible, I jumped headlong into it. And while I was occasionally frustrated by what I perceived to be my painstakingly slow progress, I also learned that surfing is one of few sports where, with the right attitude, you can be utterly abysmal and have a great time nonetheless. Still, by my second or third day out, I was managing to pop up and stand on the board regularly.

It was a perfect fit. Unlike other squadrons where football, softball, or golf are the communal activities, surfing was the pastime of choice for the Easyriders. Every Friday, the pilots and aircrew would meet at the base's White Plains Beach, where gentle waves with predictable breaks were perfect for our fledgling abilities.

Over the course of the next three years at Barbers Point, surfing became a ritual activity for me. In time I began to see my skills improve. Yet as I spent those glorious hours on my board in the idyllic waters of the South Pacific, something else happened. As my career slowly evolved alongside my surfing skills, I began to realize that while surfing had become an activity of choice when we lived near the ocean, it came to stand for something bigger, something that applied to the lives of everybody I knew, whether they had ever seen the ocean or not. For me, surfing represented *balance*, a conscious commitment to every aspect of my health and wellness, from the physical to the emotional to the spiritual. Believe it or not, it was because of this commitment to the things *outside* my work that I was able to thrive *inside* my work.

So whether your surfboard is a set of golf clubs, gardening tools, a yoga mat, or a church pew, the message rings true all the same.

Surf when you can.

After those few years at Barbers Point, surfing fell out of my life as my Navy career took me and my growing family around the world. From Hawaii we traveled to Tennessee, Texas, central California, Italy, South Carolina, San Diego, and Japan. While the opportunities to surf were relatively rare during those many years, the lessons I learned on White Plains Beach never left my side. I saw very early on that my professional responsibilities would only become more significant with time, and if I didn't take active measures to balance my life, they would eat me alive. The waves of the Pacific were thousands of miles away and my Russ-K was in storage, but the *pono* I learned from surfing in Hawaii was a lesson that stuck.

I'm sure there are lots of people who are much better at striking a balance in their lives than I am, but for the most part I think I've been pretty successful. I was always aware of the importance of balance and made it my priority to share this awareness with those around me, particularly as I rose in rank and others came to see me as an authority figure.

As the commanding officer of the USS *Blue Ridge*, one of my responsibilities was to welcome all the new chiefs to their positions. It was a big deal. The Navy has been fueled in part by the dedication and efforts of its chiefs for nearly 150 years, and attaining that rank is not something we take lightly. Chiefs are only chosen for the role after a rigorous selection process and represent a very important level of management between the senior officers and the Sailors who run a ship on a day-to-day basis.

Once first-class petty officers have been selected to be chiefs, they go through a six-week training regimen (which we call a season) designed to prepare them for the new responsibilities. The six weeks culminate with a grueling twenty-four-hour rite of passage called a "final night," followed by a formal ceremony where the new chiefs are presented in their khaki-colored uniforms and covers and officially promoted. At some point during season, the prospective chiefs and the commanding officer of the ship assemble in the Chief's Mess (dining hall), where the CO formally congratulates them on their selection and shares a few words of advice. For me, these talks were a perfect opportunity to explain what I thought it meant to be a leader.

"There are countless characteristics that define quality leadership," I would say. "But for me, five stand out among the rest. Good leaders lead; good leaders act; good leaders prioritize; good leaders mentor. And most importantly, good leaders balance family, self, and work."

This last one was always met with a few raised eyebrows. Here were twelve new chiefs sitting before me, all full of piss and vinegar and ready to tackle their newfound responsibilities with the considerable energy and talent that had gotten them there. And yet, here was the captain of the ship telling them that one of the most important things they could do was *not* work.

"Don't get me wrong," I continued. "When I'm at work, I'm all in. And we're gonna have to do some hard things together, and I'm going to ask a lot of you along the way. But at some point, everyone in this room is going to leave the Navy and you'll realize that your time here was just a small chapter in your life.

"So don't lose sight of the many things that make up who you are. When your career is over, your health, your family, and your friends will define your life. Don't think that you can turn your back on those things now and that they'll be there in ten, twenty, or thirty years. Because they won't. And I bet that by taking time off when you can, you'll also make better decisions at work, and as a result will be a better leader."

Since Barbers Point, I have come to view life as a Venn diagram, a series of three intersecting circles representing work, self, and family. Each of the three is as important as the next, and it's critical to understand where we sit in that triad.

I believe work is easy. Society dictates that most of us work for a living, and our responsibilities within those professional roles are usually pretty clear. If anything, the tendency these days is to work too much, given the pervasiveness of electronic devices in our lives. Of course, we all want to do our jobs well, be recognized for our efforts, and advance accordingly; I'm a huge believer in that. But when work has the capacity to creep into every corner of your personal life, you have to draw the line clearly and definitively.

I have always strived to be a dedicated family man, so I place the most importance on this part of the equation. As a military professional, I knew it was unreasonable to be a workaholic while in port, spend months away from family while on deployment, then expect Mary and the boys to be there for me when it was time to retire and I was finally ready to turn my attention to them. So throughout my career, I made a concerted effort to make time for my family, whether it was taking advantage of my annual leave and going away on family vacations, or setting aside time for birthdays, anniversaries, and holidays. Each one represented an opportunity for me to show the members of my family how much they meant to me, an investment that has paid for itself many times over in return.

Finally, the third circle in my diagram represents self, the one that people tend to overlook the most through the course of their lives. We can be great at our jobs and terrific at meeting the needs of our spouses and children, but how many of us truly take the time to take care of ourselves?

I'm one of those guys who go stir crazy if they don't do something active every day. Luckily for me, a Navy career is one that keeps you hopping most of the time. When I was flying fighter jets, that was usually enough excitement and adrenaline for the day. Otherwise, I needed to exercise. Whether it was running, playing softball, lifting weights in one of the carrier's six gyms while at sea, or surfing when the opportunity presented itself, I knew that I needed to move to stay physically and emotionally balanced.

We're not all built the same way. For some of us, the most fulfilling personal activity might be reading, woodworking, or playing a musical instrument. Maybe you're happiest when you walk your dog in the woods or shop for the latest fashions along a busy city street. It doesn't matter what recharges you. What matters is that you take the time to do the things that fulfill *you*. In the end, you'll be a better worker, a better leader, and a better family member.

Not too long ago, an old Navy buddy of mine called. We had worked together on the USS *Blue Ridge* but hadn't spoken in years. He had recently been remarried and wanted to share his experience with me.

"I remember when you took over command of the *Blue Ridge* and you introduced yourself to the khakis [chiefs and officers] in the wardroom," he told me. "You said the most important thing to you was your family, and keeping a healthy work-life balance. I'd never heard someone say that was their number one priority. It was the first time in my career that someone said that in order to be good at your job you had to be good at yourself and your family.

"But I didn't listen," he continued. "My first fifteen years in the Navy, I was all about the Navy. I didn't take care of myself and I didn't take care of my family. And as a result, my relationships with my wife and my kids suffered. I didn't realize it at the time, but so did my career. But I never gave up and kept looking for that balance you talked about.

"It's not always easy, but Lord knows I'm trying."

~~~~~~

The commanding officer of a Navy aircraft carrier has two cabins on the ship. The most impressive of these is the in-port cabin, a large, formal space where the CO hosts foreign dignitaries and other VIPs in grand style. As the name suggests, this cabin is typically only used when the ship is docked pierside, whether at home or in foreign waters.

While at sea, the CO spends her or his nights in a much smaller cabin just a few feet from the bridge of the ship. Utilitarian and sparse, this cabin much more accurately reflects the day-to-day life of a CO at sea. We're available, we're nearby, and we're unencumbered by extraneous distractions that might interfere with the performance of our duties.

That's done by design. The CO is ultimately responsible for everything that occurs on a ship, and having a cabin ten seconds away from the bridge makes it easier to stay involved with those occurrences when we're under way. Thanks to regular interruptions, we often sleep for only about three hours at a time (usually in a pair of sweats and a T-shirt so we can jump out of bed and get to work immediately). It's just a matter of time before the phone rings with an *extremis* situation or there's a knock at the door from someone who needs a critical question answered.

An aircraft carrier on deployment is a twenty-four-hour operation; there is always something going on. Maybe the reactor department is performing training drills and needs to inform the CO that one of the ship's two nuclear reactors will be unavailable for the next few hours. Or perhaps we're navigating on a moonless night in the vicinity of other ships—friendly or otherwise—and need to decide which course to follow to avoid confrontation or collision. The tripwires for waking the CO are everywhere . . . and they get tripped often, day and night, seven days a week.

You might think that given the crush of such responsibility, it's impossible for a CO to find time for anything other than work while at sea. I'll be the first to admit that the urge to work every minute of every day is very real. To begin with, you feel responsible for the ship, the mission, and everyone on board. On top of that, most people who rise to the position of commanding officer are driven, hardworking go-getters who like to challenge themselves and achieve success. In fact, the only way *not* to work is to make a very conscious decision and a concerted effort to pursue other interests. Doing so, of course, means knowing that by sometimes *not* working you are actually more effective when you do work. So that's exactly what I did.

On the USS *Theodore Roosevelt*, my ship's secretary was Ensign Marcello, who functioned as my right-hand man in a role very similar to that of an executive assistant in a corporation. Among other things, Marcello helped schedule my meetings, itself an onerous task since it seemed like each of the five thousand people on board the *Teddy Roosevelt* wanted a piece of my day. Add to this the fact that I had to be on the bridge for several hours each day and was still actively flying helicopters and F/A-18s as a fighter pilot, and you can see how important he was to maintaining my sanity.

Yet when I first met Marcello, I needed to make sure he understood how important it was for me to take personal time each day.

"Marcello," I said, looking at the rainbow of colored rectangles he had jammed onto the first day's schedule like Tetris, "I'm going to need some white space every day."

"White space, sir?"

"I need time between meetings to process, think, and make decisions; they can't be back to back to back."

"Understood, sir."

"Also, I'm going to need time every day for myself. Whether that's to walk the ship and talk to Sailors, work out, read, or just relax, I need you to schedule ninety minutes into each day for me to do that."

In the end, Marcello got to know me pretty well, and was as passionate about protecting my personal time as I was. There was an added benefit to my free time that Marcello perhaps didn't appreciate in the moment. The commanding officer of a ship is an important role model for every other Sailor on board. And when someone *that busy* takes time out of their schedule to ensure their personal wellness, everyone else on board begins to see the possibility, too.

I held the other senior officers on board to the same standard.

"As a leader," I said to them, "you're not just being paid to punch the clock. You are here to make big decisions. And the only way you can make big decisions is if you have time to think big thoughts. And the only way to think big thoughts is to have uninterrupted time to yourself."

In this way, I have always thought of the CO as a ship's *chief cultural officer*, the person who dictates the overall feeling and values of the ship. If I came in early, left late, worked every weekend, and never made time for myself, I knew there was going to be pressure on everyone else to do the same, whether consciously or subconsciously. On the other hand, if I showed everyone that I was willing to work hard and still make time for myself, then hopefully they would be willing to do the same.

When the ship was in port, I tried to set this example by the hours I kept. Working on a Navy ship that's deployed at sea is a twenty-four-hour-a-day, seven-day-a-week job for everyone on board. We are away from our homes, our friends, and our families for months at a time, and the work is grueling. In port, the hours are more regular. The workday starts when liberty ends at 7:00 a.m., at which point every Sailor returns to the ship from their homes and musters with their various departments and divisions.

Even then, it would have been easy for me as CO to work nonstop. But I knew that in some way the eyes of every Sailor on that ship were on me. If I came in early, they would feel compelled to do the same. If I stayed late, they would, too.

The situation was compounded by the fact that every time the CO boards or leaves a ship, it's announced to the entire crew. The Sailor serving as the bosun's mate of the watch at the ship's central watch station would sound four bells on the ship's brass bell, then announce over the 1MC intercom system either "Theodore

Roosevelt arriving!" or "Theodore Roosevelt departing!" (Traditionally, the CO of a ship always assumes the identity of the ship while on board, and his or her arrival and departure are always announced in this way.)

So it was impossible for me to quietly sneak on or off the ship. Everyone knew when I arrived and everyone knew when I left. With that in mind, I made a point of trying to arrive no earlier than 6:55 a.m. and leave no later than 4:00 p.m. In doing so, I was hoping to send a clear message to the crew: do the work you need to do and get your job done, but don't sacrifice your precious personal time along the way. If I had to accompany Mary or one of the boys to an appointment or we had planned a family vacation, I tried to go, knowing full well that I was setting an example for every other Sailor to follow.

Of course, there were times when the volume of work or special projects kept me there late, and I always did what had to be done to get the job done right. But I was never one of those people who take a briefcase full of folders home in the evenings or on weekends. As for email, I avoided it like the plague during nonwork hours, knowing that every time I sent one, the person on the other end was going to feel obligated to stop what they were doing and respond.

Sometimes my commitment to free time was more apparent than others, especially when it came to team sports, particularly softball. A rabid youth baseball player, I turned to softball in my later years, and was happy to see that loads of other Sailors shared my passion for the sport. Unfortunately, with thousands of Sailors to choose from—many of whom were good enough to play college ball—the opportunities for a guy like me to play were slim. So I formed what we called a "Khakis" team of officers and chiefs. We were strictly minor leaguers compared to the ship's A-team, but we were more interested in the exercise and camaraderie than kicking ass.

Although I always "volunteered" someone else to be captain of the team (one of the benefits of being CO), I still had a few rules. First, rank did not exist once we stepped on the field. I may have been the commanding officer of the ship, but I was just Chopper while we played. Second, we were going to practice as much as possible. This decision usually caught some of my teammates by surprise, particularly once we realized that world domination was most certainly *not* in our futures. But when I explained that practice was a great way for us to step away from the heavy professional responsibilities we all shouldered and focus on ourselves, my teammates understood.

On one occasion, we were living in Japan and I was executive officer of the USS *Ronald Reagan*. We were heavy into our softball season, had a big tournament planned for the weekend, and were making our way back to the base early one Friday morning after a few days of training exercises. As the port came into view, I knew that even though the first game didn't start for a few hours, the ship's teams would be hard-pressed to make their first game once we had taken the several hours necessary to get the ship secure to the pier. I wasn't the only one feeling the pressure.

"Sir," one of the Khakis' coaches said to me, "looks like we're going to miss the softball game, because we're pretty tight on time. The game starts in two hours and we just pulled in."

As XO, one of my many responsibilities was getting people on and off the ship once we were pierside.

"Are you guys ready to go?" I asked.

"Yes, sir. We just need to get into our uniforms."

"Well, go ahead and do that and then meet me at the quarterdeck," I said. "Once the brows are over, you'll be the first ones off the ship so you can go play."

"Really, sir? But there are another five thousand people who also want to get off the ship and begin their liberty."

"I realize that," I said, "and I also know this is important for you and your teammates. You going first won't slow anyone else down, anyway. Don't worry, I can make this work."

He and his teammates were skittish about being given preferential treatment, but I insisted. In fact, once I realized that the ship's A-team had a game scheduled for that morning, I asked the coach to have them change into their softball uniforms and assemble at the brow, too.

So there they were, two dozen Sailors and officers lined up at the *Reagan*'s brow, mitts and bats in hand, all ready to head to their upcoming games. I don't know if it's the first time a host of uniformed ballplayers ever departed first off a US Navy ship after a training exercise, but I'm pretty sure there weren't many others.

Then my radio rang. It was the ship's CO.

"Chopper, I'm assuming you have given permission for the softball teams to leave early."

"That is correct, sir," I replied. "I am letting them get off for the tournament. And sir? I'm gonna be right behind them."

"Okay, good enough, Chopper. I just wanted to make sure you're in charge."

Was I showing preferential treatment to the ballplayers (including myself)? Maybe. But nobody else on board had an issue with it. And the way I see it, I was giving preferential treatment to a life *off* the ship, which is always worth a little special consideration.

~~~~

If my wife, Mary, is my true love, then the ocean is my mistress. Ever since I was a kid, I've been fascinated with its power, its beauty, and its possibilities.

As a Navy captain, I had the privilege of experiencing the ocean in all her moods. At times it was so calm we could carve slow circles in the water with the carrier and eventually catch up with the white and blue mosaic of the ship's wake before it faded into the depths below. At other times, the sea was an unforgiving bedfellow, with waves so massive they crashed over the flight deck, sixty feet above the surface. (In some cases, fighter jets have actually been damaged by water crashing over the flight deck.)

Yet no matter what the sea threw at me over the course of those thirty years, I never stopped appreciating the perspective she offered: from my place on the bridge, with the horizon stretching forever before me, I realized just how small I was in the world.

I think that's why I have become such a staunch defender of my personal time and so passionate about surfing, or anything that lets me enjoy the ocean. No matter where you dip your toes, surfing has a way of slowing you down. It's an opportunity to disconnect from all the parts of your life—the calls, the texts, the emails, the demands, the stress—and simply *be* on the water. For me, surfing represents pressing the pause button on everything else so I can stop, look around, and breathe.

It's an egalitarian pastime as well. On the water, nobody wears a uniform, so nobody knows your rank. There are no bank accounts, no luxury cars, no economy class, and no business class. It's just you, your board, and the ocean. The journey is a personal one.

Of course, surfing is a physical undertaking, too. There are few things that compare with the feeling of freedom as you ride down the face of a perfect wave, and the exhilaration of spending a day in the sun and the water. In addition to what it offers me physically, I ultimately see surfing as a metaphor for a balanced life, one where we place as much emphasis on ourselves and our families as we do on our work.

When I have the opportunity to do something fun, I do it. Always have. Whether that was going on a family hike, taking a vacation with Mary, or heading to the water with one of our three sons, I took every chance that life threw at me, knowing it would improve everything else along the way.

The great American philosopher Ferris Bueller once said, "Life moves pretty fast. If you don't stop and look around once in a while, you could miss it."

I may not be as wise as Ferris Bueller, but I couldn't agree more. You blink and all of a sudden your kids are grown and you're retiring from a three-decade career. I guess that's why I've always assessed my life through a lens I like to call *The Rocking Chair Test*.

The Rocking Chair Test is the art of the long view. It's a perspective that helps you make decisions *now* about your life, your career, your family, and your time with an eye toward who you will be many years into the future. When you're sitting back in your rocking chair on your front porch and looking back on your life, what will you say? Which accomplishments will you be most proud of? What will you remember?

Hopefully, you'll remember lots of good things. If you're lucky, you'll look back with contentment on the scenes and stories you created. Maybe yours was a life of adventure. Maybe you chose safer ways to spend your time. Either way, the goal is to look back from your rocking chair and be satisfied with what you see. But the only way you're going to get there is if you find and take the opportunities to enjoy life.

As for me, I still surf that old Russ-K I bought back in 1995 in Barbers Point, Hawaii, but the board—like me—is beginning to show signs of age. It's covered in wax and peppered with dings and scratches, and the once-bright green triangle on the nose has faded to a dull memory. Once in a while I think of replacing it, but whenever I do, I remember that every dent tells a story, and together those stories are woven into the very fabric of my life.

When you take the time to recharge your batteries, you're giving yourself the opportunity to sharpen the blade, a blade you just might need when it's time to take a stand. Similarly, by doing something as simple as drinking espresso or playing softball, you're establishing the personal relationships that will help you pull together as a team and face the fire, whatever that may be. By embracing the hard edges and soft curves of life together, you are accepting the totality of what makes us human, and you'll likely be a better person—and leader—as a result.

CHAPTER 8

Speak Up When Things Are NKR

Seaman Thomas was as eager a young Sailor as you'd ever want to see. An Indianapolis native, he was fresh out of a three-month stint at boot camp in Great Lakes, Illinois (just outside Chicago), when he arrived on the *Theodore Roosevelt*. Like many of the newest Sailors who report to a Navy vessel for their first tour of duty, Thomas had not yet chosen a particular career path (or rate, as we call it), and came to the *TR* as an undesignated Sailor, which meant he would be assigned wherever he was needed.

Seaman Thomas ended up part of the Deck Department working as a bosun's mate, which is about as old-school as you can get on a Navy ship. One of twenty departments on the carrier, most of the ship's eighty-odd bosun's mates were young, fit, and eager. For good reason. Working on the deck team is physically demanding, and involves a lot of pulling lines, painting, and managing anchors, rescue boats, and other heavy equipment. Boatswains (whom we often call "boats" for short) also shoulder the significant responsibility of standing lookout at various points on the ship. It may seem redundant given the radar capabilities of a $10 billion aircraft carrier, but you'd be surprised how important an extra set of human eyes can be.

These watch responsibilities take bosuns to various locations on the ship, including what we call the fantail, an area just below the back end of the flight deck that offers a commanding view of the surrounding seas. When standing watch on the fantail, the bosun is in regular communication with other locations on the ship, including the bridge. We may call down to confirm the location of a boat we've picked up on radar, or the watchstander may call if he or she sees something in the water and wants to confirm that the bridge team is aware of its presence. Finally, the bosun on the fantail is responsible for reporting if anyone from the ship goes overboard.

And that's exactly where Seaman Thomas from Indianapolis found himself that night.

It was my second underway as skipper of the *TR* and we were three weeks into a major four-week certification exercise off the coast of Southern California. The ship was running at full capacity, with five-thousand-plus crew on board and an air wing of almost eighty planes and helicopters . . . and every one of us was determined to pass our final certification so we could be deployed to the Pacific.

It was a particularly calm night, rare for the waters off Southern California in early December, and dark as can be with overcast skies shrouding the moon and stars. Our fixed-wing flight ops had ended for the day (some of our MH-60R helicopters were still conducting surveillance missions), so it was relatively quiet on the fantail, at least compared to the deafening roar that typically accompanies the constant launching and landing of F/A-18 fighter jets. That's when Thomas thought he heard a splash in the water off the starboard (right) side of the ship.

It was impossible for him to be sure. It was dark, he wasn't wearing night-vision goggles, and the wake from the carrier's four screws—propellers, each weighing more than thirty tons and over twenty-five feet across—was significant, even though we were moving relatively slowly through the water. And yet Thomas thought he had seen a person in the water out of the corner of his eye. So even though he had only been a crew member on the *Theodore Roosevelt* for a couple of months and he knew the firestorm of activity he was about to set off, Thomas did exactly what he was supposed to do: he called up to the bridge to report his suspicions.

The call didn't come directly to me, but I could tell that something was going on.

"I think I've got a man overboard on the starboard side," Thomas said. "I'm pretty sure I heard a loud splash and somebody is in the water."

We knew right away that it wasn't anybody working regularly on the flight deck, because they all wear special vests that sound what's called a MOBI (Man Overboard Indicator) alarm as soon as it comes in contact with salt water. The MOBI also sets off a flashing light and emits a radio signal that can be tracked from the bridge and traced back to a specific Sailor on the ship.

We didn't see any MOBI-related indications, but that didn't completely allay our fears. Anybody else could have fallen in, whether they were walking along the catwalk on either side of the ship or had gotten too close to the edge of the flight deck, lost their balance, and plummeted to the water fifty-five feet below. Another possibility, though grim, was that someone from the crew intentionally jumped.

Despite the lack of indication from our MOBIs, the watch-stander was insistent. He felt confident that one of his fellow Sailors was in the water and needed our help. That was all we needed to hear.

"Sir," the senior bosun's mate on the bridge said to me as he held the radio to his ear, "the aft lookout thinks we have a Sailor in the water."

"Call it away," I said.

The bridge team leapt into action, blowing three shrill whistles over the 1MC, a Navy tradition that sounds an emergency and is designed to bring everyone on board to attention, whether they're sleeping or awake.

"Man overboard! Man overboard! Man overboard, starboard side! All hands muster for report!" they called over the 1MC. A minute later, they did it again.

When this type of alarm is called, every person on the ship is required to immediately assemble—no matter what they're doing at the time—at a predesignated area with the other members of their division, and then report the results of that muster to their parent department or squadron. This allows every person on board to be accounted for. It's a time-consuming process (even as captain I had to be accounted for), but it's the only way to make sure that nobody is in the water. Once we've accounted for every Sailor, the man overboard muster is called off and life on the ship returns to normal.

In the meantime, every other nonessential activity on the ship stops and the carrier's entire focus becomes finding the person in the water. It's a vast ocean, and even though the Sailor may be relatively near the ship, it's still incredibly difficult to spot someone against such a massive backdrop—especially in the dark of night.

Luckily, Thomas followed procedures and threw what we call a "smoke" in the water as soon as he heard the suspicious splash. A smoke is a floating, water-activated cylindrical marker that emits a slow, steady stream of white smoke and flame for close to an hour. The smoke may not be in the exact position where the Sailor fell in, but it gives those of us on the ship a relative idea of where to look. And with the ocean stretching endlessly toward the horizon, any visual clue is welcome.

Nevertheless, we didn't wait for the report from the ship-wide muster before beginning the search in earnest. We slowed the *TR* to a crawl and began to slowly circle back to the spot marked by the smoke. At the same time we launched two additional MH-60S helicopters off the flight deck, which immediately began to circle low over the area, search lights shining brightly on the water below as the pilots looked out from the cockpit and rescue swimmers in the back of the helicopter leaned over the sides to scan the waters below.

Fifteen minutes later, we got the report from the full ship-wide muster: one Sailor was unaccounted for.

Wow, I thought. *The kid was right.*

Every set of eyes on the bridge was glued to the waters below. In the air, the helicopters circled low, the chop of their rotors buffeting the waters below. As soon as the muster was complete,

Sailors from across the *TR* began to make their way to the flight deck and starboard side of the hangar bay that opened to the ocean; it wasn't long before there were hundreds of them on the starboard side of the ship searching for their shipmate.

Moments later, one of the helicopter pilots radioed the bridge.

"Captain," he said, "I think I've got something in the water. We're going to drop down to take a closer look."

A few minutes later, the helicopter crew radioed back with news that they had been unable to locate anyone. It didn't ease our fears much, because someone falling from the catwalk or flight deck plummets five stories before hitting the water and could easily be knocked unconscious. There are several scenarios for what happens after that, and none of them are good.

After a bit more time had passed, we called for a second muster. This time, every Sailor on board the *Theodore Roosevelt* was present and accounted for. (Turns out the missing person during the first muster was nothing more than a Sailor who had fallen asleep in her rack while wearing noise-canceling headphones.) I kept the helicopters in the air for another thirty minutes just to be safe, but when they found no sign of anything in the water, I called off the search.

Then I called for Seaman Thomas to come to the bridge.

It was a long walk from the fantail to the bridge where I waited for him, and I'm sure the twelve flights of stairs he had to climb gave him lots of time to think about the heap of trouble he was about to get into. Not only that, but here was a nineteen-year-old kid just out of boot camp being called to the bridge by the ship's CO. Needless to say, Thomas was terrified by the time he made it to the bridge: not only had he brought a $10 billion aircraft carrier of five thousand people to a screeching halt, but he had done so in the midst of a series of very important certification exercises.

He approached timidly, then saluted. "Good evening, sir," he said while standing at attention.

"Hey, bud," I replied. "How are you doing?"

"Good, sir," he replied, unable to meet my gaze and looking down at his feet.

Unable to contain himself, he jumped to the explanation that he'd obviously been preparing for the previous ten minutes.

"Sir, I swear I heard a loud splash," he began. "It sounded big enough to be a body or something and I was worried someone fell off the flight deck. I looked over and thought I saw something, but it was dark enough that I couldn't see for certain. So I called the bridge and then threw the smoke over to mark the spot."

This time he held my gaze, though I could almost hear his knees knocking.

"You know what?" I said. "You did *exactly* what I wanted you to do. The fact that there wasn't anyone in the water is immaterial to me. You did the right thing, and I can sleep better at night knowing people like you will have the strength of conviction to report something when they see it."

His face exploded into a smile and he breathed a sigh of relief.

Then I reached into my pocket and handed him one of the command coins I had made when I was named CO of the *Theodore Roosevelt*. Rather than a captain's ego trip, command coins are a military tradition meant to serve as reward and motivation for the ship's crew, many of whom have never been to the bridge of a ship or met a commanding officer. Two inches in diameter, my coins had the *Teddy Roosevelt*'s logo on one side and a large command star with my name around the edge on the other.

"Thanks," I said as I handed it to him and shook his hand warmly. "Thanks for being a good shipmate and thanks for keeping an eye on your fellow Sailors."

"Thank you, sir!" he said, smiling broadly.

In doing so—in rewarding a teenager for his decisive actions instead of berating him for overreacting—I was hoping that my message would ripple throughout the thousands of other Sailors on the ship. As it turns out, the person Seaman Thomas thought had fallen into the water ended up being a wooden crate that somebody on the flight deck had moved and had later been blown over the side by jet wash from an aircraft conducting maintenance. But to me, it didn't matter.

What mattered was that Sailor Thomas had chosen to put himself out there and communicate his concerns despite his junior rank and the significant implications of his actions. Sure, it was just a wooden box that ultimately would sink to the ocean floor, but had it been a Sailor, Thomas's actions may very well have saved someone's life.

And if that's not motivation to communicate fearlessly, I don't know what is.

~~~~~~

The four reactor engineering spaces of a US Navy *Nimitz*-class aircraft carrier are intimidating places. Each one is almost as large as a high school basketball gym and responsible for generating every ounce of power used during the vessel's operations, from the ship's propulsion to the steam that powers the four catapults that launch our aircraft.

(Each catapult is approximately three hundred feet long, a steel cylinder situated just under the surface of the flight deck that shoots a "shuttle" from one end to the other with frightening force. The shuttle is attached to the launch bar on an aircraft, and as the shuttle accelerates down the flight deck it takes the aircraft with it, allowing it to go from 0 to 150 mph in just over two seconds before launching off the bow of the ship.)

Reactors are the heart of an aircraft carrier, and the five hundred members of the Reactor Department are charged with the significant responsibility of keeping it all running smoothly, twenty-four hours a day, seven days a week, 365 days a year. (The Reactor Department also uses distillation to desalinate sea water and produce the approximately 400,000 gallons of fresh water used on the ship *every day*, essentially making it a city-sized power- and water-generation department.)

Yet for all the switches, dials, valves, wheels, and complex technology that characterize the Reactor Room, it is the two active nuclear reactors and their associated operating equipment that stretch across its entire length that have made it a space to be respected—perhaps even honored—by Sailors since the world's first nuclear-powered aircraft carrier, the USS *Enterprise*, was commissioned on November 25, 1961. The two A4W nuclear reactors that power and propel the Navy's *Nimitz*-class aircraft carriers are extraordinarily complex machines. Rated at approximately 550 thermal megawatts, each reactor generates enough steam to produce approximately 140,000 shaft horsepower for a pair of the ship's four propulsion shafts plus 100 megawatts of electricity used throughout the ship.

Needless to say, the Sailors who choose to make their careers as reactor engineers ("nukes," for short) play a vital role in the safety and battleworthiness of the ship, whether they're crusty twenty-five-year veterans of the Navy or twenty-year-old junior Sailors fresh out of the Navy's Nuclear Power School and heading to sea for the first time. Yet irrespective of the number of deployments these Sailors have under their belts or the number of lines on their faces, there's one critical trait they all share: from the moment Sailors express interest in pursuing nuclear engineering as their Navy specialty, they're taught the value of open, honest, and unguarded communication, and the vital role that it plays in maintaining the integrity of the reactors and the safety of everyone on board the ship.

It's a mantra that becomes immediately apparent to anyone who has ever spent time in the department. Much like pilots discussing their flights, the Reactor Department is an egalitarian setting, one where everyone has equal input and nobody's thoughts or opinions are disregarded.

Attend a Reactor Department brief or debrief and—aside from the mountains of insanely technical language they bat around like teenage slang—you quickly see this philosophy in action. Everyone is subject to the same level of scrutiny and analysis as everyone else, regardless of rank or seniority. In other places on the ship, a senior lieutenant commander who makes a mistake while speaking might not necessarily be corrected on his error, and certainly not by junior Sailors. In the Reactor Department, however, such niceties do not exist.

In fact, reactor engineers are trained to speak up every time they see or hear something that's even the slightest bit off base, because they know what's at stake.

"I'm sorry, sir, but that's incorrect," one might say to her *very* superior officer. "The correct pressure limit is one five zero pounds, not one seven zero pounds."

It's a fascinating phenomenon, and one that is mimicked in few other places in any branch of the military. And while some crusty Navy veterans may have been put off by the apparent brashness of the Reactor Department's young engineers, I always found it healthy and refreshing. What's more, it reinforced my core belief that speaking the truth—particularly in a situation when lives might be at stake—is far more important than rigid adherence to hierarchy and rank. Empowering people to communicate freely is vital to the success of any organization. But giving people the freedom to communicate *fearlessly*—even when others may not necessarily be expecting or wanting their opinion—is what distinguishes a good organization from a great one.

I tried to encourage Reactor Department–type communication throughout my career and was always on the lookout for ways to share this message with the Sailors and officers around me. This was especially important to me during what we call "special evolutions" in the Navy, high-stakes operations that require special effort and coordination among the various departments of the ship. An evolution can comprise anything from docking at a foreign port to pulling alongside another ship to exchange fuel and ammunition. Yet no matter what the nature of the exercise, evolutions all have one thing in common: briefings.

The briefing session for a special evolution is a critical piece of the puzzle and can last anywhere from thirty to ninety minutes. During these sessions, the representatives of the ship's many departments each have an opportunity to discuss the role their department will play in the exercise, and we would all go over the sequence of events as well as the areas we considered high risk. I would always close out the briefing so I could hit the high points, and invariably I would end each one by reiterating what I thought to be the most vital message of all.

"Remember that I need everyone in this room and every Sailor on board this ship to play their part," I said. "So don't think you're a passive participant in this. You're not a fan in the stadium; you're on the field playing. So if you see something that's NKR—Not Quite Right—I need you to speak up."

The first few times I dropped this intentional faux pas into the speech, nobody corrected me (I'm not the world's greatest speller, but I do know that the word *quite* begins with a *q* and not a *k*!) . . . which is exactly why I continued to do it in subsequent iterations. If these department heads didn't believe enough in themselves to correct me when I made a blatant error, how would they react in an *extremis* situation? I suspect it's because they knew I was trying to make a point, but it was important for me that someone stood up to me, even if I was the CO. For me, it's not enough that a high-performing organization encourage dissenting opinions. It must expect it and build a culture that allows even the most junior member to speak up when something seems out of line.

Eventually someone gathered up the courage.

"Excuse me, sir," said Petty Officer Barnes, who had just recently reported to the *Roosevelt*, "but you realize Not Quite Right is actually abbreviated NQR, right, not NKR?" He grinned.

"So it is, Petty Officer Barnes," I said as I returned the smile.

From that point on, NKR became a calling card for open, unguarded communication on all the ships under my command. (I'd like to say I pioneered the concept, but once again it was something I learned from my great mentor, Bolter.) From then on, every time I brought it up during a briefing, someone would either correct me or the entire room would break into laughter. Still, while the delivery may have been humorous, there was nothing funny about the message, and everybody recognized the difference.

In time, the NKR concept spread to every corner of the ship and served as a constant reminder to all our Sailors that speaking up was an expectation, no matter how innocuous the situation may have seemed or how junior their rank. I'm not saying we ever got to the point where the entire ship functioned like the Reactor Department, but I like to think we got pretty darn close.

~~~~~

The US Navy base in Guam has played an important role in our country's history for nearly eight decades. Although the island has been occupied by different nations throughout the years, it officially became a US territory on July 21, 1944, when American troops liberated it from Japanese control after three weeks of bloody battle.

Since then, Naval Base Guam has served as a foundation for American strategic operations throughout the Pacific. The base played a major role during both the Korean War and Vietnam War, and today supports Navy actions in the area in a variety of ways. Throw in the fact that one in every eight adults in Guam has served in the US armed forces and you can see why military support there is so strong. I had the pleasure of visiting the friendly tropical island many times during my Navy career, but few proved as memorable as 2004, when a rookie pilot's failure to communicate almost cost me my life.

At the time, I was a department head assigned to VFA-94, and one of the senior fighter pilots on the USS *Nimitz*, which was operating approximately 150 miles off the coast of Guam en route to the Persian Gulf for combat missions in Iraq. On the day in question, I was scheduled to train one of the squadron's junior pilots, call sign Casper, on the use of night-vision goggles (NVGs) during combat missions.

As part of the exercise, Casper would also practice using the jet's forward-looking infrared cameras (FLIRs) to locate a variety of geographic landmarks on the island, which I was going to select for him throughout the course of the flight. Anything from old bunkers to bridges to parking lots, these landmarks would serve as dummy targets during the mission, allowing the pilot a chance to fine-tune his FLIR target acquisition skills while still competently flying the jet. Missions like this are common during pilot training and occur virtually anywhere the Navy has a base (I've "targeted" gas stations on interstate I-5 more times than people filling up below would care to know). Luckily for all parties involved, we never carry ordnance during these flights.

Although our training plan called for us to launch off and ultimately return to the *Nimitz*, being so close to Guam afforded us an extra level of security: if something went wrong, we would have Andersen Air Force Base on the island as an alternative landing site. It was very unlikely we'd need the backup, but as with any night mission, it was nice to have the option. (Legend has it that the Navy did a study during the Vietnam era where pilots were connected to a variety of heart monitors and blood pressure monitors, then tested for their physiologic responses during combat. When the data were analyzed, it was found that landing on a carrier at night elicited twice the amount of stressful responses as flying in actual combat missions over Hanoi.)

After we launched from the ship, Casper and I separated by ten miles, as our training plan dictated. From that distance I fed him a series of dummy targets around the island, which he located using his FLIR. After about thirty minutes of this, satisfied that he was competent in the use of the equipment, we regrouped and prepared to head back to the ship.

With the two planes now flying in formation, protocol called for us to perform visual inspections of each other's jets from approximately ten feet away using our NVGs before making our way back to the *Nimitz*, some 150 miles to the southwest. These inspections, which we call battle-damage checks, allow pilots to examine and assess their wingman's planes for anything out of the ordinary, such as damage from combat or malfunctioning equipment. While we didn't expect any damage in this case, we still practiced the maneuver as if we had just returned from an actual combat mission.

"Snake, fence out," I said over the radio to Casper using our section call sign. (This was the command I gave that directed the rest of the flight, in this case telling Casper to turn off all unnecessary combat-type equipment and switches in his jet and closely look over my jet.)

As part of this dialogue, pilots flying in a section or division (two or four jets flying in formation together) always perform standard fuel checks with one another, once the battle-damage checks are complete.

"Snake 61, upjet 7.0," I said, meaning my jet had no issues and I had 7,000 pounds of gas (approximately 1,050 gallons) remaining.

"Snake 62, upjet 7.8," Casper replied.

Although it was unusual that my fuel level was 800 pounds lower than Casper's, I wasn't overly concerned. As I've said, fuel consumption on an F/A-18 varies greatly according to how the jet is flown. Maybe I was flying around a little bit more or faster than normal while he was practicing with his FLIR or perhaps I just got a little careless with my throttle and was burning more gas than normal. Either way, I still had plenty of fuel for the return trip and landing.

When a fighter jet lands on an aircraft carrier at sea, the weight of the aircraft is important, and the amount of fuel on board the jet is a critical part of the calculation. With too much fuel on board, the jet will exceed its maximum landing weight of approximately 45,000 pounds, which can result in possible damage to the landing gear. On the other hand, pilots have to make sure they have enough fuel in case they don't land on their first pass and have to fly around and try again. So we always want to be on the upper end of the weight scale on landing, without exceeding our maximum.

Casper and I continued to press on toward the *Nimitz*. When we got within about thirty miles, I checked in with the approach controllers who work in the air traffic control center on board. That's when I noticed that my fuel level had dropped down even faster than it otherwise should have. A fighter jet typically burns approximately 1,500 pounds of fuel every fifteen minutes, yet in the fifteen minutes that had elapsed since Casper and I had done our battle-damage checks, I had burned an additional 2,000. My fuel level was now at 5.0 . . . and dropping.

It didn't make any sense. I double-checked my math. There were no indications of a fuel leak or any kind of engine malfunction. To make sure, I closely examined the jet's fuel-dump switch, which controls the plane's ability to release excess fuel when necessary. Fortunately, I was still comfortably above the amount of fuel I needed to make it back to the ship and land safely on my first trap.

When we had closed to within five minutes of the *Nimitz*, I began to shoot my approach (since I was lower on fuel, I would land first, followed by Casper approximately two minutes behind me). Fuel was becoming a real concern, and it was beginning to drop faster with every second. I had been doing calculations in my head all along, and—even accounting for my increased fuel consumption—I should have been at 4.5. I was now at 4.0.

At this point I was convinced the jet had some sort of fuel leak, but it seemed manageable enough that I was still going to land with more than 3.5, the minimum recommended amount for a night trap. I was wary, but confident that even if I got caught in the barrel I would have enough fuel to meet up with a tanker or get back to Guam, if need be.

When I was less than three minutes from landing, I did another fuel calculation in my head, only to find that my rate of fuel loss had grown exponentially greater. In this scenario—at night and over 150 miles away from Guam—a fighter jet should never land with a fuel level below 3.0, which we still consider *extremis*. As I approached the ship with less than a minute to go, I watched my fuel level drop swiftly through that.

At that point, my world became very small. I knew I only had one option. If I tried to do anything but land, I was going to run out of gas. I couldn't go find the tanker and I couldn't return to Guam, because I didn't have enough fuel for either. To make matters worse, my fuel state was so low that I would only have one shot at landing on the flight deck. In the dark. If I missed, the only option would be to pull up and away from the ship, have the jet flame out (run out of gas), and then shell out (eject) into the water below, destroying the airplane and forcing me to take an unwanted open-ocean, late-night swim.

With less than thirty seconds to landing, the controllers calmly gave me their last call, which helped temper the growing chaos in my cockpit.

"Four oh five," they said smoothly, "three-quarters of a mile, on and on. Call the ball." (Translation: Aircraft number 405, you're on glideslope and on centerline for your final approach to landing; tell the landing signal officers [LSO] you see the ball and report your fuel state.)

"Four oh five, Hornet ball," I replied. "Two point five," referring to my lower-than-optimum fuel state.

The next call would be from the lead LSO, a pilot whose job when not flying was to position himself or herself at the back end of the ship and provide the final radio calls necessary to ensure jets safely land on the flight deck. I figured my fuel state would set off major alarm bells with the LSO, especially because I had communicated it with him a few minutes earlier and he certainly would not have been expecting it to drop so dramatically in the few minutes that had elapsed. But either he misheard me, thought I messed up the call, or realized that my real fuel state was so low that I had no choice but to land and had better not add any stress to what I was already feeling. Either way, he remained incredibly calm. So rather than say something like, "What?" or "Sorry, 405, repeat your fuel level," the LSO quickly and calmly replied. "Roger, ball. You're looking good."

In thirty years of a Navy career, I don't think I ever felt quite as focused as I did during those excruciatingly long final seconds of approach to the flight deck. One screwup, one missed wire, and things would get really bad really quickly. Breathing as deeply and steadily as I could, I focused on the "ball" just to the left of the landing area and the centerline lights of the flight deck and called upon every ounce of my training as I flew smoothly downward for my trap: meatball, lineup, angle of attack. Thankfully, my tailhook grabbed the three-wire and the jet quickly came to a stop on the flight deck.

As I was rolling out (taxiing) to clear the landing area for Casper, the air boss called me on the radio.

"Hey, 405," he said, "looks like you've got your dumps on." (Translation: You're dumping fuel onto the flight deck.)

"Boss, I'm pretty sure I have a fuel leak," I replied. "I'll shut it down once I'm clear of the landing area."

Once I was chocked and chained (meaning the jet was firmly connected to the flight deck and couldn't move), I quickly shut down the jet, unstrapped from the ejection seat, and climbed out of the cockpit. As I looked back over my shoulder, I saw a large puddle of JP-5 fuel growing under the jet. Seconds later, the flight deck crash crew (specially trained aircraft firefighters) sprayed fire-retardant foam on the area to prevent any possible fire. Shortly after they had cleaned off the flight deck, Casper landed without incident.

A maintenance crew then arrived on the scene, trying to figure out what had gone wrong. Turns out one of the jet's main fuel lines had ruptured in flight and was spitting fuel everywhere. Later, as I met with the squadron maintenance chief to log my hours and go over the flight before heading to the debrief, he explained what had happened.

"Sir," he said, "you're lucky. That was a big leak, and it must have gotten even bigger from vibrations throughout the flight. Your jet could have easily run out of fuel or caught fire."

Still hyperfocused from the adrenaline pumping through my system but thankful for the guardian angel that had been watching over me, I headed to the debrief room, where Casper and I went over the flight. I told him what had happened, along with the report I had received from the maintenance team.

"That makes sense," he said, "because when I did the battle-damage check I thought I saw something. I was on NVGs for the first time, but looking back at it, there was fuel mist coming from under your jet. It didn't make sense, but I didn't think it was anything abnormal. I'm sorry; I should have said something becau—"

"Wait . . . what?" I interrupted. I tried to remember that he was a junior pilot who didn't have a lot of hours and was flying with NVGs for the first time. Still, given my apparent brush with death, I felt the urge to strangle him. For a moment, anyway. Then I fell back on my training, which stresses the vital importance of pilots to maintain their composure in every possible situation.

As pilots, we're taught from the day we start flight school that if we ever find ourselves in a life-or-death situation, there are far more important things to focus on than the fear of death. To do otherwise means you're losing precious seconds, time you could be spending thinking about how to get yourself out of the situation. If it's already happened—as it had in this case—then it can't kill you anymore, so you don't worry about it.

Believe me, it would have been easy to lose my cool. But I recognized in the moment that there was nothing to be gained by doing so, for me or Casper. I calmed myself and spoke again.

"Casper," I said, "if you had simply told me that something abnormal was coming out of my jet, it would have been all I needed to confirm that I had a fuel leak earlier in the flight. And then I would have just gone and landed in Guam, and avoided all this. So, yes, it would have been cool if you said something."

I could tell by the look on his face that he was embarrassed by the situation and regretted not saying anything at the time.

"I think at the end of the day we can both learn from this experience," I said. "If we see something, we have to believe in ourselves enough to say something. It's as simple as that."

I had vented as much as my training and personality would allow. It was time for both of us to move on.

Throughout the rest of my career, every time I briefed a flight, I'd end it by saying, "If you see something that doesn't look right, no matter how insignificant or innocuous it may seem, your responsibility to yourself and to your other pilots is to say something.

"The worst thing that can happen is that you point something out and it's not an issue," I continued. "But the best case is you might save an airplane and you might save your wingman's life."

~~~~~~

Though the roots of the Hans Christian Andersen tale are murky, the moral behind "The Emperor's New Clothes" is one that has withstood the test of time. As the story goes, an extraordinarily vain emperor was hoodwinked by a pair of swindlers who sold him an outfit so rare and magnificent that it could only be seen by the most capable and competent among his ranks. Although a succession of his most trusted aides checked on the progress of the "weavers," none was confident enough to report the trickery to the emperor, for fear of being thought incompetent or incapable by the monarch. When the emperor finally addressed his subjects in his new "outfit," the townspeople also went along with the ruse for fear of appearing stupid. In fact, it wasn't until a child cried out that the emperor was parading around in his underwear that the truth eventually came out.

Life isn't always as simple as Andersen would have us believe. We've got mortgages to pay, children to raise, spouses to answer to. In some ways, then, the decisions we make are not solely our own, since their ripple effects can stir the waters for many people in our lives. I understand that, and I'm not naïve enough to think that everyone is going to speak up every time they get the itch, because the consequences of these actions can sometimes be severe.

To further complicate matters, these kinds of decisions are never black-and-white, but more like a couple hundred shades of gray. I agree it's a bit crazy to bring the entire ship to a halt because a single widget is in the wrong place. But sometimes that misplaced widget might actually be the thing that puts the life of someone else—maybe more than one person—in danger. In those cases—like a Sailor falling overboard or a jet spraying fuel—I'd like to believe that people have enough of a compass to know that things have crossed into the red zone and could get very bad, very quickly.

You may never find yourself in that position. You may never have to stare down the barrel of a gun and know you're putting your career on the line to take care of others. I never thought I would have to, either. But when you do—when the stakes become dangerously high for everyone involved, when you realize things are NKR and you have the confidence to speak up anyway—it can be one of the most important things you'll ever do.

CHAPTER 9

Take a Stand

It was only 8:30 in the evening, but I was tired. More tired, I think, than I had ever been since finishing the Navy's SERE (Survival, Evasion, Resistance, and Escape) school twenty-five years earlier. I had only slept for a couple of hours over the previous three days, but as commanding officer of a US Navy vessel, I had become accustomed to the occasional all-nighter. This time, though, my exhaustion was different.

Sitting there at my desk in what felt like the dead of night, I stared bleary-eyed at the blue-white glow of the computer screen. Before me was the email I had written to several senior officers in my chain of command expressing my grave concerns over a situation that had the potential to claim more of my Sailors' lives than any combat scenario I had been involved with over the previous thirty years: SARS-CoV-2 (COVID-19).

I hadn't gotten there quickly, rashly, or easily. The number of COVID-19 cases on the USS *Theodore Roosevelt* had grown steadily over the previous seven days, and I knew that if decisive action were not immediately taken to stem its transmission, we would soon be sitting on a full-fledged outbreak. And on a ship of five thousand Sailors—all living, working, sleeping, eating, and playing in close contact—the virus would spread like a California wildfire.

I read the email over and over again. I fact-checked it. I questioned it. I edited it. I didn't want to step out of line and knew the message had the potential to ruffle more than a few feathers. But if I needed to raise a few eyebrows to convey the gravity of our situation and spur my superiors to action, then that's what I was going to do.

I addressed the email to a total of ten people—three admirals and their three personal assistants, along with four senior officers on the *Teddy Roosevelt*—less than a dozen action-oriented officers in my chain of command, all of whom were in positions to help.

Over the one-page email and attached four-page analysis, I outlined the situation on the ship, the inadequate measures that had been made to that point to contain it, our go-forward needs, and a plan to address it. While I was comforted by the knowledge that many of the other senior officers on the *Theodore Roosevelt* had reviewed my email and were willing to sign their names alongside mine, I knew full well the risk I was taking by asking for help in this way.

I fully realize that I bear responsibility for not demanding more decisive action the moment we pulled in, but at this point my only priority is the continued well-being of the crew and embarked staff. As you know,

*the accountability of a Commanding Officer is absolute,
and I believe if there is ever a time to ask for help it is
now regardless of the impact on my career.*

*Vr [very respectfully],
Chopper*

It was 8:48 p.m. on March 29, 2020, in Guam. I read the email one last time, then clicked Send.

Four days later, I was removed from command by the acting secretary of the Navy and left the ship for the last time.

~~~~~

On December 31, 2019, the Wuhan Municipal Health Commission in Wuhan, China, reported a cluster of unique pneumonia cases that had never been seen before. The World Health Organization described the cases as being of "unknown etiology," meaning their cause was a mystery. As we know now, those forty-four mysterious cases of pneumonia heralded the beginning of the COVID-19 pandemic. For me it signaled the beginning of the end of my tenure as captain of the USS *Theodore Roosevelt*, and ultimately, my thirty-year career in the US Navy.

But the story of my dismissal from the *Teddy Roosevelt* doesn't begin on that New Year's Eve. It started two years earlier, in 2017, when I was named commanding officer of the USS *Blue Ridge*.

We were stationed at the US naval base in Yokosuka, Japan, where the *Blue Ridge* and her crew were based. Then, on June 17, as I was attending an event in Tokyo with Mary and two of our three sons, Sean and Ian, I received a call from the ship: there had been a collision at sea between the USS *Fitzgerald* and a local merchant ship. Lives had been lost.

"We're not sure what happened, Captain, but the *Fitzgerald* is coming back to port, and the base has asked us to provide Sailors who can be there to help when she pulls in."

"I'm on my way," I said.

I would soon learn that the *Fitzgerald* had collided with a container ship flying under the Philippine flag some eighty nautical miles southwest of Tokyo. The *Fitzgerald* was trying to maneuver the busy waters around Tokyo Bay at night and found itself in front of the container ship, unable to get out of the way. The container ship rammed directly into the *Fitzgerald* broadside, flooding several of the lower berthing spaces, injuring three and killing seven Sailors, whose bodies were later recovered from the flooded compartments. There were no reported injuries on the container ship.

Late the next evening, I stood on the pier in the dark and watched as the *Fitzgerald* was towed in by several tugs, the once-mighty 510-foot destroyer listing to its side like a wounded animal. The 350-odd Sailors who disembarked from the ship had stunned looks on their faces, as though they could not believe what had happened to their ship and their shipmates.

A couple of weeks later, the surviving members of the *Fitzgerald*, along with everyone on base, held a memorial for the seven fallen Sailors, many of whom had family living with them in Japan at the time. Hundreds of us lined the streets, holding American flags and paying tribute to the dead as their families made their way from the base's chapel to a local auditorium where the memorial service was going to be held. It was a solemn, heartbreaking moment I'll never forget.

In the subsequent investigation, we learned that in addition to a series of mistakes made at the time of the collision, the *Fitzgerald* was also overtasked and unprepared to go to sea. The ship wasn't adequately manned and had been working under an extremely hectic schedule. The crew had been working an unusually long day, were extremely tired, and made mistakes in the busiest of waterways, which ultimately cost them dearly. I have no doubt that the *Fitzgerald*'s commanding officer—who was ultimately responsible for the safety and well-being of his Sailors—wishes he had pushed back against the overwhelming burden of operational tasks he received from headquarters, and spoken up when his crew needed a break.

In the end, the two senior officers and the top enlisted Sailors on the ship were all relieved of duty for the roles they played in the accident; several others on board were also punished for their errors. For the Navy, it was the beginning of what was going to turn out to be a tragic summer, one that painfully highlighted the importance of taking a stand when necessary for the well-being of those that you have been entrusted to lead.

Fast-forward two months to August 21, when the warship USS *John S. McCain* was involved in a nearly identical incident, this time with the Liberian-flagged tanker called the *Alnic MC* off the coast of Singapore and Malaysia. The *McCain* was operating in dense traffic in a busy channel, somehow got sideways, and was hit broadside by the *Alnic*. The breach resulted in flooding to nearby compartments, killing ten Sailors.

Following the *McCain* collision, I was selected to fly to Singapore, along with a Navy lawyer and a few other officers, to lead a portion of the investigation into the incident. And if I thought the *Fitzgerald* experience was sobering, dealing with the *McCain* was far more intense for me, if only because my level of involvement was that much greater.

After arriving in Singapore, we spent some time talking with the ship's commanding officer and executive officer. We walked the ship and saw the compartments where the Sailors had been trapped after the collision. Through our investigations, we learned that the *McCain* had been in a situation very similar to that of the *Fitzgerald*. The crew was overworked, and Sailors who stood critical watch stations on the bridge were not adequately trained; some had been shoved into position at the last minute.

It wasn't like the Sailors were completely unprepared for the job. They had been qualified to stand watch on other ships, but the equipment they were asked to operate on the *McCain* was slightly different than what they were accustomed to, and some had yet to be officially certified in its use (even though it's a requirement before standing watch). Those subtle differences led to a series of errors and misunderstandings that ultimately caused the ship to lose steering control, get sideways, and get rammed by the *Alnic*.

As with the *Fitzgerald*, the CO and XO of the *McCain* were held accountable for the collision and relieved of duty. Interestingly, the Navy also fired the Seventh Fleet's commander at the time, a vice admiral. Subsequent investigations saw even more officers lose their positions because of the two accidents.

In the end, those investigations always came back to one thing: the commanding officers on the ships accepted risk where they didn't have to, didn't speak up when they could have, and didn't take decisive action when they should have. The mistakes that were made were the product of many people not speaking up when something was NKR, and as a result, seventeen Sailors died.

~~~~~

It was against this backdrop of preventable tragedy that I had taken command of the *Blue Ridge*. And while I didn't know any of the Sailors on the *Fitzgerald* or *McCain* personally, I took their deaths to heart. These were men and women whom I had likely seen on the naval base in Yokosuka, passed on the pier on the way to work, or saluted and wished a good day. And now they were gone. I resolved then that something like that would never happen to my Sailors, and I would always heed the words of Chief Garcia from so many years before:

Take care of your Sailors.

Take care of your Sailors.

Take care of your Sailors.

With that in mind, I resolved that my first priority in every noncombat situation would be the safety and well-being of my Sailors above all else. If anybody tried to push us past those limits, I would push back. If I needed to say no, I would say no. It was my responsibility to my Sailors, my ship, and my Navy.

A few years later, this lesson would resonate acutely. Taking a stand for what you believe in sometimes comes at the cost of pissing people off and risking personal advancement, but I hoped that I'd always have the courage to speak up when I saw something wrong rather than be the person giving the memorial for those entrusted to my care.

~~~~~

In November 2019, I was honored to assume control as the captain of the USS *Theodore Roosevelt* aircraft carrier, the thousand-foot wrecking machine that is the envy of the world's naval forces. For a career Navy man, becoming commander of the *TR* was the culmination of a lifelong dream. Not only did I find myself at the helm of one of the most powerful ships ever constructed, but I had also been entrusted with the well-being of the five thousand crew on board.

In January 2020, after a couple of months of maintenance on the ship and at-sea training with the crew, we were ready for deployment. Personally, I felt ready as well: I was comfortable driving the ship, had come to know the Sailors on board, and felt confident I could lead them with honor and purpose. As we set out to deploy on January 17, I felt like we were ready for anything.

"Look behind me," I told the press from the pier in San Diego. "You see a thousand feet of American warship, the most powerful ship in the Navy, ready to go, and sharp as a knife. But don't be fooled by the missile systems, the fighter jets, and the steel. Because what you don't see behind me are the five thousand Sailors that call this ship home. They're what makes this ship truly formidable."

Yet even as we left the pier, brimming with enthusiasm, our departure was somewhat clouded by something that had recently begun to be reported on the news: a yet-unnamed virus emerging in China.

The months to come would also prove to be the ultimate test of all my experience to that point, a time when I was forced to call upon every lesson in life and leadership I had previously learned. From relationships to kindness, prioritizing to teamwork, this would be the crucible where it all came together. And even though my actions ultimately led to me losing my command,

I stand by what I did, and I know that my decisions ultimately made things better for all Sailors across the Navy.

~~~~~

The *TR* sailed west toward our destination in the South China Sea. The ship was running well, and every day I got to know the department heads, the officers, and the Sailors better. In addition to being the commanding officer of the ship, I remained current as a pilot, and flew F/A-18 E/F fighter jets and MH-60 helicopters in training missions every few days.

We made our first port call in Guam in early February. We'd been on the ship for more than three weeks, and everyone enjoyed some well-deserved liberty on the tropical island. Sailors played golf, enjoyed the beaches, and relaxed in local hotels. As the CO, I was proud that there were no incidents of Sailor misconduct during our stay, not an easy feat given the size of our crew. On February 5, we left Guam.

By that point, the COVID-19 situation in the world had changed markedly, and we had begun to pay quite a bit more attention to the virus. Of particular interest to us were reports of a Princess Cruises vessel that had been refused entry into Japan because of an outbreak on the ship. COVID-19 was on our minds.

As we sailed west from Guam over the course of the next few weeks, the Chinese navy was our constant companion, maintaining a respectful but watchful eye on us from two or three miles away. Our plan was to operate in the South China Sea throughout February, arriving in Vietnam in early March.

About ten days before our Vietnam port call, we started paying very close attention to COVID-19. The virus was beginning to gain a foothold in Southeast Asia, and people were dying. By most accounts, the fatality rate was 4 or 5 percent, though older people seemed to be at greatest risk. Even so, we were keeping a watchful eye on Vietnam, since our crew would undoubtedly enjoy themselves in local bars and hotels, and on beaches. At that point, the term *social distancing* didn't even exist.

Despite our concerns, we received no direction from the Navy to alter course, so we anchored in Da Nang Harbor, Vietnam, on March 5. The visit was scheduled to commemorate the twenty-fifth anniversary of US-Vietnamese diplomatic relations, and apparently no one at the senior levels of government wanted to cancel it. Nevertheless, the other commanders and I had decided to limit our Sailors' interactions onshore as much as feasible. We also chose to restrict the number of Vietnamese officials and guests we hosted on board. As a final precaution, we began to screen Sailors for flu-like symptoms, and if necessary take the temperature of everyone who went on and off the ship.

For the most part, the Sailors and Vietnamese rolled their eyes at us, because Vietnam reportedly had very few active cases of COVID-19. I suspected that might have been because very little testing was taking place, so we decided to play it safe nonetheless. We continued to limit exposure as much as we could and monitor the local situation, and we were prepared to adjust our plan accordingly should anything change. From the Navy's standpoint, though, it was business as usual, with many high-profile events attended by senior officials scheduled to take place. Our first day in port there was a big reception on the pier, followed the next night by a party attended by some four hundred people at a hotel. The party was initially scheduled to be on the *TR*, but due to poor weather, rough seas, and the concern about COVID-19, I decided to move the event ashore to the Danang Golden Bay Hotel, where the ship and crew would be less at risk.

I was hoping to relax in Da Nang as well. Mary had even planned on flying in for a visit but changed her mind a few days before departing because of COVID's spread through Asia. To make the most of what remained of the port call, a few other officers and I planned on surfing in Da Nang the day before we were scheduled to depart. It never happened.

~~~~~

At around 1:00 a.m. on March 8, the liaison officer from the US embassy in Hanoi—who was in Da Nang to help coordinate our visit—called to tell us that two British nationals in Da Nang for a golf vacation had tested positive for COVID-19. The Vietnamese government wanted to quarantine the entire Vanda Hotel, and thirty-nine Sailors were staying there: thirty from the *TR*, plus another nine from other ships in the strike group that were also in port. Because the *TR* had more space and better medical care, we would eventually put all thirty-nine on board the carrier in quarantine while we monitored them for signs of COVID.

After speaking with our very experienced senior medical officer, Captain John York (a Navy doctor), on the *TR* as well as the ship's XO, we decided to set up a command post in downtown Da Nang to plan our next steps. It was a touchy situation, as the Vietnamese government didn't want to let our Sailors leave. I had no intention of leaving them behind, but at the same time I was concerned about possible spread of the virus to other Sailors. (Although the Vietnam War had ended decades earlier, I didn't think it was appropriate to leave US Navy Sailors in Da Nang under Vietnamese government control.)

We decided to test the Sailors in question and quarantine them in the hotel for the remainder of our stay, as well as on board once we returned to the ship. This was in the very early days of the virus, and we didn't have the luxury of the rapid tests that became available many months later. Each test was far more involved and took anywhere from ten to twelve hours to culture results. Fortunately, we had flown an epidemiology team on board, and they dedicated all their efforts to COVID-19. Even so, they were still limited to two hundred tests per day.

Fortunately, all the Sailors at the Vanda Hotel tested negative for COVID. But not wanting to take any chances, I ordered them all quarantined in an isolated berthing space once they returned to the ship. With only thirty-nine to worry about, we could easily isolate them in areas away from the rest of the crew.

The plan was to check them daily for symptoms, bring them their meals, and keep them away from the thousands of other people on board. Based on guidance from the US Centers for Disease Control and Prevention (CDC) at the time, we would test them again two weeks later. Those who tested negative would be released back to their duties.

At the same time, much of the world was also starting to battle COVID-19. Hospital rooms were filling up in most major cities, there were worldwide shortages of ventilators and masks, and the number of positive cases and COVID-related deaths was growing exponentially.

The *TR* left Da Nang on March 9 with those thirty-nine Sailors in quarantine. On board the ship, we were doing our best with limited space and supplies to wage our own battle with COVID-19. We increased the number of what we called *bleach-a-paloozas*, set times when everyone on board was tasked with wiping down common surfaces with a diluted bleach spray. In lieu of the masks we didn't have, we eventually authorized everyone to wear their "flash gear," a protective hood and gloves issued to every Sailor in case of fire on the ship. The hood can be fashioned in such a way that it almost functions as a mask . . . almost. Ultimately, the image of our Sailors wearing flash gear and wiping down surfaces during bleach-a-paloozas became more common than we ever would have suspected at the start of deployment.

We also began social distancing and asked Sailors to stay six feet apart from one another, recognizing full well that it was nearly impossible to do that in the cramped quarters of the ship. All things considered, we felt as though we had a pretty good handle on the situation. We had quarantined the Sailors in question and were taking extensive sanitary precautions throughout the ship.

On March 22—two weeks after they had initially tested positive for the virus—the thirty-nine Sailors in quarantine were retested; all tested negative and were released back to the crew. Personally, I felt like we had dodged a very large bullet. I had no idea what lay ahead in the days and weeks to come.

~~~~~

Given the irregular and often-interrupted sleep that characterizes a commanding officer's typical night, I didn't think anything was out of the ordinary when my phone rang at 2:00 a.m. on March 23. Until I realized it was our Senior Medical Officer Captain John York.

"Captain, two Sailors just tested positive for COVID-19," he said. "And we think there's a third one as well."

Oh, hell.

Somewhere in the back of my mind, I knew this was the moment that would change everything. We'd had about twenty-four hours to enjoy the notion that we'd escaped disaster in Vietnam, only to realize we hadn't been so lucky. The three Sailors who had just tested positive were not part of the initial quarantined group and had therefore been interacting freely throughout the ship. To make matters worse, we could only test a couple hundred Sailors each day. It would take almost a month to test the entire crew. We quickly quarantined the three Sailors and started doing close-contact tracing.

I called the strike group admiral and let him know what was happening. My immediate boss in the Navy hierarchy, the one-star strike group admiral was responsible for all the ships in the strike group, including the flagship aircraft carrier, a couple of destroyers and cruisers, as well as our air squadrons, in total the better part of seven thousand men and women strong.

As predicted, the number of positive cases began to climb as our testing continued. On March 25, there were four confirmed cases on board. By March 26, that number had risen to somewhere between twenty-five and thirty-three. We hadn't yet reached the point where the spread was exponential, but it certainly seemed to be headed in that direction. Plus, we knew there were more positive cases on board that had yet to be confirmed. The brutal fact of the matter was that we simply didn't have enough tests and couldn't utilize the tests we had on board as quickly as we wanted to because they were so cumbersome and time-consuming.

Given this stark reality, we started limiting activities and access on board the *TR* as of midmorning. All social gatherings were restricted, the ship's buffet lines (the only way you can feed five thousand people three-plus meals a day) were changed to service only, and the gyms had strict limits on numbers. We didn't shut everything down, but we were moving that way. Meanwhile, we quickly shelved our plan to dock in Thailand and decided instead to return to Guam, where it would be easier for us to handle whatever was about to be thrown at us. As we got closer to Guam, we were able to start flying COVID-positive Sailors ashore to remove them from the ship and get them care at Naval Hospital Guam.

~~~~~

As the number of cases on board the ship continued to climb, so did my sense of urgency. That feeling, however, did not seem to be shared by the senior leadership ashore. There were lots of meetings and videoconferences every day with senior staff off ship—including the three-star Seventh Fleet admiral back in Japan and the Pacific Fleet commander, a four-star admiral based in Hawaii—but very little action otherwise.

For my part, all I cared about was mitigating the COVID risk on board and getting the *Roosevelt* safely to Guam, where we could spread out and start getting people off the ship. Since there was no modeling at the time to show how the virus might spread on the *TR*, we used the *Diamond Princess* cruise ship as our primary case study. Here was a luxury vessel where most parties had their own stateroom with a private bathroom—yet they still had a massive outbreak, with at least twelve fatalities. By comparison, I was commanding a densely packed aircraft carrier where shared quarters and bathrooms were the rule, not the exception.

And while we didn't have the luxury of exploring numerous different plans and options, I knew that if we didn't take immediate action, we were going to have several thousand people test positive. With a global fatality rate of approximately 4 percent, we were looking at the potential for dozens of deaths.

To be fair, we didn't think our fatality rate would be nearly as high as that recorded among the general public. A Navy aircraft carrier is overwhelmingly staffed with young, healthy, fit people. So we projected a worst-case fatality rate on the *TR* of 1 percent, 75 percent less than the current global rate, and 50 percent less than the *Diamond Princess*. But even 1 percent of a thousand infected Sailors would mean ten fatalities, which was ten too many in my book (and nobody had even heard of long COVID back then).

Meanwhile, the government's maddeningly slow responses continued. The Seventh Fleet and Pacific Fleet, which together are in charge of every US naval craft in the Pacific, told us they were examining other possibilities, including sending the *TR* to Japan, Hawaii, or even back to San Diego. I have no doubt they were also answering to their bosses back in Washington, DC, but the micromanagement by the highest levels of the government was making it almost impossible to take any swift action on board.

For example, we were asked to determine how many of the *TR*'s Sailors smoked, while we had already come up with a priority list of those that we wanted to get off the ship immediately based on existing medical conditions and key watch-standing requirements. After we painstakingly accounted for all our smokers, we were then asked by headquarters to determine how many

Sailors "vaped" in addition to smoking cigarettes. It didn't matter that vaping was no longer allowed on board US Navy ships; somewhere someone thought this was vital information to be recorded. Of course, when Sailors learned that vaping might allow them to leave the ship more quickly, suddenly almost 50 percent of the crew had instantly taken up the habit.

This disconnect between the front lines and senior decision makers is sometimes referred to as the fog of war, a phenomenon that often occurs in dynamic and quickly evolving situations. On the *Teddy Roosevelt*, we were completely in tune with what was happening on board, including our ever-growing infection rate and the challenges we faced in keeping Sailors socially distanced. The Seventh Fleet was a few days behind with respect to understanding what was happening on board, their bosses another few days behind that, and officials in DC another three or four days behind that yet again.

The same thing happens when you micromanage in combat. If the soldier on the front lines needs permission to take action from his boss and his boss's boss and his boss's boss's boss, it's never going to happen in time for that soldier to make a difference. That's exactly what we were experiencing on the *TR*. We were ready to take action, but folks kept putting up barriers that slowed us down.

Our situation certainly wasn't helped by the acting secretary of the Navy at the time, Thomas Modly, who told the governor of Guam that the *TR* didn't need any help once we reached port. In retrospect, Modly's comments were far from the truth: COVID was spreading fast among the Sailors, and we needed all the help we could get to obtain adequate space ashore.

To his credit, Modly reached out to me through his chief of

staff shortly after the *TR* had pulled into Guam's Apra Harbor and asked how he could help.

"I need more CDC-compliant spaces ashore," I told him. "I need individual rooms for my Sailors to prevent the spread of COVID."

It was obvious to me that we needed rooms that complied with CDC recommendations, preferably individual rooms for each Sailor, with its own bathroom. Modly told me he would help, but with the caveat that we would confine ourselves to the base. I imagine Modly's comments were influenced by the administration's generally cavalier attitude regarding COVID, which saw the president regularly downplaying the seriousness of the virus. On the ship, however, we were witnessing firsthand how quickly the virus could spread when proper spaces were unavailable.

We finally pulled into Guam on March 27, with thirty-six confirmed cases of COVID-19 on board. Although we started moving Sailors off the ship as quickly as we could, it wasn't fast enough. By midday on March 28, our positive COVID cases had grown to 44, then to 46 later that evening. By the evening of March 29, we had 53 positive cases on board. Worse yet, another 1,000 Sailors who were deemed "close contact" to those who had tested positive were in "quarantine" on the ship.

We prioritized those infected with the virus and sent them to various sites on base to receive medical care and be quarantined there. For the rest, the Navy had retrofitted a few of the gyms on the base into makeshift accommodations, where rows of cots would house hundreds of Sailors. Every day we had hundreds of Sailors, sea bags slung over their shoulders, waiting in the hangar bay for hours to be moved to on-base facilities. Given the conflicting guidance we were receiving from our higher-ups about testing requirements, our offloading of Sailors to the (less-than-adequate) facilities ashore slowed to a crawl. On many of those days, we had to tell the Sailors to return to their racks on board and we'd try again the next.

It didn't take an epidemiologist to realize that the large on-base facilities set aside for the Sailors were not going to help the situation. Sure, some of our Sailors would be off the ship as space became available, but they would still be in close contact with one another, including largely shared bathrooms and showers. All things considered, it wasn't much of an improvement over what we had on the *TR*, and it was an unacceptable long-term solution.

The senior Navy leadership off the *TR* was clearly trying to come to grips with the problem, but they were stuck in a bureaucratic process that seemed to be trying to balance operational needs and ever-changing medical advice from numerous off-ship senior officials. It was frustrating. I don't know how many times we were given conflicting guidance or told, "We'll have another meeting tomorrow to talk about it and look at options."

By the morning of March 29, 2020, I realized I was at a crossroads. I could go along with the Navy's variable testing requirements and clearly ineffective plan to house the Sailors in close contact with each other around the base, and hope it all worked out in the end (even though we knew it wouldn't), or I could stand up for what I knew was right, cut through the bureaucracy to ensure that Navy leadership understood the problem, and fight to ensure the Sailors were getting the best care possible given the challenging situation. We would move them off the ship as quickly as we could into the available gyms, but they needed to know that this would not be an acceptable long-term solution.

Take care of your Sailors.

After running several different scenarios, we decided that the best long-term course of action was to take advantage of hotels across the island. Guam had approximately ten thousand rooms available, and most of them were empty at the time because tourist traffic had been shut down. Yes, it would cost a few million dollars (chump change compared to the Department of Defense's total budget of almost $700 billion) to house thousands of Sailors for up to fourteen days. But if that saved one Sailor's life, then it was money well spent. Unfortunately, I didn't have the authority to make it happen and couldn't legally sign a contract for use of the hotels that we needed.

~~~~~

In the hours that followed, I crafted my email, along with an accompanying four-page letter explicitly requesting assistance, proposing the hotel solution, and describing how we would continue to take care of the ship while in port. I also explained that we could quickly bring Sailors back on board and set sail, should world events require it. I knew my perceived frustration would ruffle some feathers and I would very likely take some heat from my higher-ups as a result. On the other hand, I was confident it would get the ball moving and immediately clear up some of the fog of war.

As Alexander Hamilton once said, "If you don't stand for something, you'll fall for anything." And I knew my Sailors were worth standing up for.

When the email was done, I asked several of the *TR*'s senior officers on board to review it, to make sure I wasn't overreacting. None thought I was, and to a man they believed it to be the right course of action. In fact, a few of them asked if I wanted them to sign as well. I said no, for several reasons. First, I didn't want anyone else to take responsibility for my words. Second, I didn't want the Navy brass to think we were all conspiring against them. Finally, I was confident I was doing the right thing by bringing attention to the situation and was okay taking the heat if the Navy wanted to push back.

The Sailors were always my priority. Helping the Navy solve the problem on board as quickly as possible was the intent behind my request for assistance. Following the accidents with the *Fitzgerald* and the *McCain*, there had been significant blowback on the Navy. So even if I would take the hit within the Navy, I figured that at least the Navy wouldn't get hammered for inaction from the public.

~~~~~

Shortly after I sent the email, the strike group admiral on board the *TR* came to my office to talk. He was surprised to find me there with the majority of the other captains from the *TR*, with whom I had conferred before sending the email.

"Chopper, why did you send that?" he asked. "Why didn't you ask me first?"

"Had I asked you," I said, "there was a chance you would have told me not to send it. Then my dilemma would have been to disobey you and send it anyway, which I would have done. I wanted you to have deniability so you could tell your bosses you had no idea that I was going to send it. But if I didn't send this and we don't do something right now, this is going to get further out of control. And then we're all going to be held accountable because Sailors died and we didn't take action quickly enough."

The first off-ship response I received came early the following morning, from the air boss, the admiral in San Diego in charge of all US naval aviation. His tone was positive, and exactly what we were hoping for.

"Hey, Chopper," he said, "thanks for the red flare. We're going to get you the help you need."

The reaction from the other admirals was very different.

"Chopper!" one wrote. "Call me ASAP!"

Was it the right thing to do? I still believe it was. In fact, the use of hotels to quarantine Sailors before and during deployments went on to become standard practice across the Navy. At the same time, I also realize I made it difficult for my bosses to support our efforts to take care of the Sailors of the *TR* without looking like they were merely reacting to my plea. I have no doubt that Navy leadership at the time cared about the well-being of *TR* Sailors, but I also knew they were removed from the situation on board and there was no way they cared about them as much as I did.

If I had to do it all over again, knowing only what we did at the time I sent it, I'd like to I believe I'd do it. It was a privilege to be the commanding officer of one of the greatest vessels in the history of modern warfare. But if I wasn't willing to take a stand for my Sailors even if it meant potentially sacrificing my career, then I wasn't qualified to lead them from the beginning.

On March 31, my email was leaked to the *San Francisco Chronicle*. Although I never wrote the email with the intention of seeing it published, I knew full well the risks inherent in using an unclassified network to send the email: it would have been extremely easy for anyone on that distribution list to forward the email to their own personal address, then send it along to whomever they wanted from the safety of their home network. That said, my decision to use the unclassified network was reasonable. To that point *all* our COVID-related communications had been over unclassified networks because most Navy medical officials don't have access to the classified networks. I was simply following the same path everyone in the Navy had already been using, and I wanted to ensure that Navy medical professionals could be kept informed of the gravity of the situation.

Nevertheless, the leaked email represented a critical turning point in the evolution of the event, and that's when the potential impact to my career became clear. I even joked with one of the other warfare commanders on board that my days were numbered.

"Are you kidding, Chopper?" he said. "They can't fire you now. They'd look like fools if they did."

Almost immediately, my communications with military leadership began to change. A call I was scheduled to have with then secretary of defense Mark Esper the following day was abruptly canceled. Emails I received from Modly's chief of staff had a markedly different tone; suddenly they seemed very lawyerly, and very specifically began to reference offers of help that he had apparently made previously.

I don't know if Modly went into the press conference the next day believing that I had leaked the letter, but he clearly misstated the facts by claiming that I sent my email to twenty or thirty people and raised alarm bells unnecessarily. His unfortunate reaction to my request for assistance would quickly bring an end to my command, and impact him negatively as well.

Nonetheless, my email kick-started some long-needed action. Suddenly there was a sense of urgency from the Navy brass that had been lacking to that point. By April 1, four thousand hotel rooms in Guam had been obtained, so we were able to quickly start getting significant numbers of Sailors off the ship and into proper accommodations . . . while simultaneously writing the procedures for the rest of the Navy on how to deal with COVID-19 in the future.

~~~~~

On the morning of April 3 in Guam, my phone rang while I was in the shower. I was exhausted, felt terrible, and was worried I might have COVID (which, as it turns out, I did). It was the strike group admiral on board.

"Hey, Chopper, I need to talk to you in my office."

Moments later I walked into his office, where he was waiting with the chief of staff.

"Chopper, I've just been directed by the acting secretary of the Navy to relieve you of command of the USS *Theodore Roosevelt*," he said, a clear tone of compassion in his voice. "I need you to work with the XO so he can assume command before you leave the ship. But I'd like you to leave the ship today."

And that was it. It was April 3, 2020, and my thirty-year career in the Navy was coming to an end.

After everything I had been through over the course of those three decades, it all seemed a bit surreal. For as long as I could remember, the Navy was my family. I had forged lifelong friendships, seen my peers killed in the line of duty, and watched my boys grow up in cities around the world as a result. And now, it was over.

I guess I should have seen it coming. As time went on and the microscope focused ever more sharply on the issue, I realized the Navy was finding itself in an increasingly difficult position. If they came to my aid, it would seem like they were kowtowing to the whims of a rogue captain. Nonetheless, I had allowed myself to be overly encouraged by the initial response from the Navy that they were going to give me what I needed to do my job and protect the Sailors. I was wrong.

"Sir," I said, "I'm sure I'll have questions later, but I know it doesn't matter right now. I appreciate you telling me in person and I'll be off the ship by the end of the day."

I returned to my room to start packing. The first thing I did was call Mary to tell her what had happened, but before I could even get the words out, she said, "I'm so sorry, hun. It's already in the news."

Shortly thereafter I gathered my department heads and told them what happened. Interestingly, a lot of them had already heard the news, too, which shows how quickly even so-called classified information can make its way around a ship. Either way, there were tears, fist bumps, and hugs. I told them I stood by my actions and was confident I had done what was required to take care of our Sailors. Surprisingly, their reactions were far stronger than my own. They were angry. They were sad. They were mournful. In the end, I reminded them that there was more work to be done.

"You've got to fight on," I said. "The Sailors are our priority, and they're counting on you."

~~~~~

As news of my firing spread on board, a constant stream of Sailors came by my room to pay their respects and say goodbye. Later that night, I was finally ready to leave the ship for the last time.

A US aircraft carrier typically has two gangplanks, or what we call *brows*: an officers' brow, used exclusively by officers and chiefs, which leads to the ceremonial quarterdeck, and a Sailors' brow. The officers' brow typically closes at six o'clock each night, so rather than have to open it up again, I chose to leave the ship via the Sailors' brow. I had no idea what awaited me.

When I stepped onto the hangar bay that leads to the brow, I was met with a sight that will stay with me for the rest of my life. Standing there at full attention were more than two thousand Sailors, plus another thousand Sailors around the flight deck looking down.

The main body of Sailors had created a path for me to walk through at a comfortable distance. And while the specter of COVID was certainly hanging over everyone's heads (we still didn't have enough masks for the crew), it didn't seem to matter in that instance. Trying to keep my distance as best I could, I walked the massive, silent gauntlet of Sailors. I recognized most of them and couldn't help but think of the incredible times we had spent sailing across the Pacific, launching and recovering airplanes and helicopters, or enjoying liberty in foreign ports.

Once I had passed through and reached the hangar elevator, the Sailors broke ranks and started cheering. It was a heck of a sendoff and highlighted the magnitude of what we were all going through. For me, it demonstrated that standing up for my beliefs mattered . . . to the people who mattered.

My first step from the ship to the brow felt heavier than normal as I recalled the events of the previous few days, and the last couple of months in command of the *TR*. I paused to take in the scene on the hanger bay and flight deck one final time, saluted the crew, turned, and slowly walked off the ship for the last time. It was the evening of April 3, 2020, and the most memorable day of my thirty-year Navy career. I have not been back on board since, but I will never forget the ship and the Sailors whom I was lucky enough to serve with.

~~~~~

What happened after that was a goat rope. I was set to spend the next month in a guest cabin on the base in Guam while I recovered from COVID.

My cell number somehow got out into the public and my phone began to ring almost immediately, and rarely stopped. I only spoke with Mary or a few close friends, and until my retirement I never made a statement to the press or gave a public interview. It was a conscious decision because I didn't want my firing to become a national debate for the Navy and distract from getting care to the *TR*'s Sailors.

Unfortunately, the media attention became a distraction anyway . . . at least for Navy leadership. In the ensuing media firestorm, the press blasted the Navy for how it handled the situation, particularly Acting Secretary Modly, who made some pretty disparaging remarks about me in the press and on board the *TR*.

Interestingly, I received a surprise visit from Modly while I was still on the base in Guam. The region admiral, my temporary neighbor in Guam, knocked on my door on the morning of April 6.

"Hey, Chopper, the SECNAV [acting Secretary of the Navy] would like to speak with you."

"No problem," I said. "When should I call?"

"Chopper, he's actually waiting outside."

Unshaven and unprepared, I went outside unmasked (we didn't even have enough for the crew, let alone a now-fired captain) in my shorts, polo shirt, and flip-flops, a very different appearance than that of Modly in his N-95 mask and wearing dress slacks, button-up shirt, and blue jacket bearing a large SECNAV patch on the chest. Over the next thirty minutes we talked at length about the situation, though with a comfortable six-foot gap between us.

To Modly's credit, he cordially asked how I was doing, and said he thought I could have been clearer in my initial communications. At the same time, he spent a lot of time lamenting how badly he and the administration were being treated in the press, and how biased he felt the coverage of the situation had been.

In retrospect, what struck me most about our conversation was how frustrated and overwhelmed he seemed by the events that had taken place. At one point he took a couple of deep breaths and told me point-blank that he would always keep his comments professional and would never attack me personally.

"Thanks, sir," I said. "This is not a personal thing. I think we're both trying to do what's right for the Sailors and the Navy, even though we might have disagreed on the best way forward."

No sooner had I returned to my cabin and turned on the TV than I saw Modly's visit to the ship earlier in the day being broadcast on the news. Addressing the Sailors over the 1MC, Modly came across as clearly angry at the crew, and made a series of disparaging personal comments about me (one of the Sailors recorded Modly's tirade, which ironically found its way to social media and then the mainstream news). Almost immediately after he returned to Washington after visiting the *TR*, Modly was asked to resign by Congress, which he did. I have no doubt that he wanted what was best for the Navy and the administration, and it was unfortunate in the end that he got caught up in the situation and made mistakes that cost him his career.

Do I disagree with the acting secretary of the Navy's decision to relieve me of duty? Yes. But at the same time, I understand why he made it. In the end, he was doing what he thought was best for the Navy, which was his responsibility, just as I was doing what I thought was best for the Sailors on the *Roosevelt*.

The weeks that followed were equally tumultuous. On April 14, I received a call from the office of the chief of naval operations (CNO) in Washington, DC, telling me they had looked over the preliminary investigation into the incident and were going to recommend I be reinstated. The plan at that point was that I'd go back to the ship as soon as I was cleared of COVID, finish deployment, and bring it back home to San Diego.

It was a good conversation, and the admirals I spoke with acknowledged that the decision to fire me had been made in haste and in the fog of war. At the same time, I recognized the precedent they were setting: no commanding officer in Navy history had ever been relieved of command (and none relieved directly by the SECNAV) and subsequently reinstated. As excited as I was about my possible reinstatement, I was also encouraged for the Navy, because I believed the move demonstrated its public commitment to admitting mistakes, learning from them, and growing as an organization.

As soon as the call ended, I started working with a great Navy public affairs officer to write a statement that would be released to the press after my reinstatement, which was scheduled for Thursday, April 16.

April 16 came and went, and nothing happened. Then, on Friday, April 17, I finally got a call from the same admiral in the CNO's office. He told me that the secretary of defense disagreed with the Navy's recommendation and felt that a more thorough investigation was needed. My reinstatement was on hold for at least a few weeks, if not months.

With my life in an uncomfortable state of limbo, the vice admiral in San Diego recommended that I return home to be with my family while I awaited the CNO's decision. Upon reinstatement, I would be flown back to the *TR* to finish our deployment. Ten days later I was cleared of COVID and flew back home on a commercial flight.

~~~~~~

The next two months were challenging as I waited for word, but I was glad to be home with Mary and the boys. Finally, on June 19, 2020, the CNO's office released a statement saying it had completed its investigation and concluded that as CO I had not done enough to properly mitigate the risk of COVID on board the *TR*, particularly once we were in Guam.

They went on to say they believed I actually held out for hotel space in Guam and did not take advantage of the limited space that was made available for the Sailors on the base. The *TR*'s strike group admiral was also implicated in the investigation and would unfortunately not receive the promotion that would have seen him receive a second star and be assigned another important position within the Navy.

Just as I had in Guam, I went from the high of expecting I would be reinstated to the crashing reality that it wouldn't happen. Only this time I knew it was permanent. And while I stand by my actions, it was a difficult realization nonetheless. Until that point, including the morning of the announcement, everyone believed that I was going to be reinstated. My phone call with the vice chief of naval operations was brief.

"Hey, Chopper," he said, "we've taken a close look, and the bottom line is the CNO is not going to recommend reinstatement based on the results of the investigation."

As disheartened as I was, I was not angry, nor did I dispute the decision. In some ways, my reaction was very similar to that after Casper had failed to tell me my jet was leaking fuel all those years before. Tempered by my career as a pilot and trained to be as cool as possible under even the most *extremis* situations, I did not blow up when I got the news. Believe it or not, I recognized in that moment that there was nothing to be gained by raising a stink. Instead, the predominant emotion I felt at the time was disappointment. I believed in my heart that reinstatement was the right thing for me as well as the crew I had represented. Yet what mattered most to me in that moment was what had mattered to me throughout the experience: how the crew was going to be taken care of.

"I'm sure it wasn't an easy decision for the CNO, but I appreciate the heads-up, sir," I said.

The San Diego vice admiral offered me a job on the spot as one of his senior directors, a position I held until my retirement almost two years later. I am forever grateful to him for that, along with the support he and his wife gave to me and Mary throughout the saga.

In the weeks and months that followed, I had the opportunity to review and reflect on the events and subsequent investigation. More than anything, I was rankled by the fact that the investigation took issue not with my email, but rather with the steps taken by me and the rest of the crew to mitigate, contain, and deal with the COVID once it was on board. From the beginning, our priorities were to protect the crew, preserve our fighting capability, and get back to sea as soon as we could. The remaining leaders and Sailors on the *TR* did just that, and after only a couple of weeks in Guam had returned the ship back to sea, where they conducted flight operations and continued their mission.

To a person, the crew of the *Theodore Roosevelt* busted their asses, day and night, to take care of the ship and each other. From the medical team that continued to take phenomenal care of their shipmates, to the public affairs teams dealing with thousands of press inquiries, to the Sailors who cleaned the ship and had to figure out how to get safely under way, every person on board did far more than could ever have been expected of them.

Among its many criticisms, the Navy said we didn't take appropriate action to protect and socially distance Sailors on board when we could, and for insisting on CDC-compliant hotel rooms as the ideal solution. Anyone who has ever been on an aircraft carrier knows it is virtually impossible to keep Sailors apart when many of them live in berthing spaces that hold over two hundred Sailors, all sleeping and living within a few feet of one another. The Navy also said we didn't adequately mask the crew, but they failed to acknowledge that we (like the rest of the world) were short supplied and simply didn't have enough for everyone on board (and even resorted to using flash gear as makeshift masks).

The investigation—based on limited information born of interviews performed by videoconferencing two months after the fact and from thousands of miles away—also concluded that we had released people from quarantine when we shouldn't have. What they failed to recognize is that we weren't putting Sailors in quarantine if they *tested positive* (we didn't have enough tests to make a dent in the crew), but if they were in close contact with someone else who *had* tested positive. Well, it quickly became obvious—and our contact tracing proved—that virtually everyone on board had been in close contact in one way or another with a positive case, so quarantining was an exercise in futility. Even so, we took whatever steps we could on board to maximize social distancing.

Finally, the Navy criticized us for not getting Sailors off the ship as quickly as possible. In reality, however, we shuttled Sailors ashore constantly once we pulled into Guam, and were sending them for quarantine on base as quickly as they could be accepted.

Despite any positive impact the email may have had by shining a light on the situation on board and prompting the Navy to action, the incident ultimately had the negative effect I was hoping it wouldn't: it made the Navy look bad. After I was relieved of duty, the Navy was left trying to explain why it had fired someone who took a stand on behalf of the Sailors when their lives were at stake. I am certain that everyone in the Navy believes what I stated in my initial email: "If we don't act now, we are failing to take care of our most important asset, our Sailors." We just disagreed on how quickly that action needed to be taken.

At the same time, I also realize that my methods weren't perfect. I should have been more adamant and clearer to senior leaders at the outset about how dire the situation was and how concerned I was for the well-being of my Sailors. Maybe I should also have put more trust in the chain of command to solve the problem, as I have no doubt they also didn't want to see any Sailors die from COVID-19.

Shortly after I learned I would not be reinstated, I had the opportunity to speak with a US congresswoman who reached out to see how I was doing. During that conversation, she revealed that the new secretary of the Navy had made his decision because I had acted with my heart instead of my head. I told her I disagreed, but if that was the worst accusation he had for me, I could live with it.

Nevertheless, a good leader is ultimately responsible for what happens under his or her watch. I owned it, was responsible for what happened on the *TR*, and therefore was obligated to stand up to protect the crew when it was required. And if the result of that decisive action helped the crew but made me lose my job, I'm okay with that.

I guess you could argue that in some ways I let the crew down, because getting myself fired meant I wasn't there to finish the fight alongside them. And you'd probably be right. As the saying goes, there is no cause worth dying for that isn't better served by living to fight on. So the downside of me being removed is that

I left the crew on their own, so to speak (though in very capable hands). For despite everything I had tried to model about team-work, camaraderie, loyalty, and trust, in the end I wasn't there.

On the other hand, I always believed my first priority as CO was to take care of the Sailors. That didn't mean I had the luxury of changing or sacrificing my values as soon as things got tough. If I was going to be true to my beliefs, then it meant standing up for them even if I might be punished as a result.

So what did I gain in the end? I gained the knowledge that I had the strength of conviction to take a stand for what I believed in. What was important to me before the outbreak remained equally important to me thereafter. Hopefully the crew recog-nized that I was a man of my word. After all the speeches and stories and anecdotes, I showed them how I operated under fire.

Believe me, it would have been easy to rationalize *not* doing what I did and simply work within the confines of big Navy's system. But at the same time, I would have been tacitly accepting risks to my crew, even though they had no say in the matter. I wasn't going to do that.

Is that breaking rank, or is it just being true to your values? In the end, I believe it's the latter. And if being true to my values means I broke rank, so be it. Because the way I see it, rank isn't as important as being true to yourself and the people you've sworn to take care of.

~~~~~

In early July 2020, the USS *Theodore Roosevelt* returned from its tumultuous deployment to clear skies and a sunny Naval Air Sta-tion North Island in San Diego. It was a warm, gorgeous Southern

California morning, so a good friend (and former *TR* XO) and I took our paddleboards about a half mile off Coronado to watch her arrive. As we floated there and saw all the Sailors in uniform standing along the edge of the flight deck ceremonially "manning the rails," I reflected on everything that had happened over the course of the previous five months.

In the end, there were more than 1,200 positive cases of COVID-19 on the ship, and one death, a low number when you consider the millions who died around the world as a result of the virus, but still one death too many. That man, forty-one-year-old Aviation Ordnanceman Chief Petty Officer Charles Robert Thacker Jr., left behind a wife and two children who expected and deserved to have him in their lives for many years to come.

I will never forget Chief Thacker or the entire *TR* crew, but I know in my heart we did everything we could to keep those Sailors safe and healthy. I took a stand for the people I was responsible for and lucky enough to lead. I may have lost my job as a result, but I feel good knowing that when faced with a challenging situation with many lives at stake, I chose to take care of my Sailors rather than to protect my career.

That's the great lesson from my time in the Navy. We can move through life on the path of least resistance, hoping others will take the lead when tough decisions need to be made. But by standing up for what you believe in, standing up for the well-being of others regardless of the personal consequences . . . that's where true character can be forged.

Epilogue

On the morning of March 26, 2022, a picture-perfect spring day in San Diego, my retirement ceremony from the US Navy was held on the deck of the USS *Midway*, the legendary aircraft carrier that operated for forty-seven years between her commissioning eight days after the end of World War II and her decommissioning in 1992. As I stood there before the gathering of some 350 people—family, friends, shipmates, and colleagues I had served with through hell and fire over the previous thirty years—particularly my sister Becky, who made the trip despite being in the midst of a three-year battle with cancer—it struck me that although I had joined the Navy to fly, I had stayed for the people.

People I served with, deployed with, flew with, surfed with, and went to war with. People I worked for, and at times, people I was privileged to lead. Looking out over that crowd of familiar faces, I was comfortable in the knowledge that after three decades of service, my faith in people had never wavered, and they had never let me down. And when those people serve as part of a larger organization like the Navy—where they're valued both as individuals and as part of a team—they can accomplish anything, and defeat any foe. Even though I was removed from my command of the USS *Theodore Roosevelt* by the Navy, the organization remained loyal to me and my family to the end. As I've always said, the Navy is a family business . . . *our* family's business.

Almost immediately after I learned that I would not be reinstated as CO of the *TR*, the vice admiral in San Diego hired me as the director of Naval Aviation Readiness, an important position that had me oversee all 179 Navy air squadrons and a multibillion-dollar budget used for everything from training rookie pilots to preparing airwings for deployment. It was a far-reaching job with significant responsibility, and I was fortunate to work with a staff of two dozen experts, top-notch men and women from the helicopter, fighter, and patrol communities.

One of the best parts of the job was that it allowed me to continue to fly fighter jets, only this time as an instructor in Lemoore. For one week each month, I would spend my days teaching rookie nugget pilots in F/A-18s I had first flown there more than two decades before. In some cases I was in the backseat for their first-ever flight in a Navy tactical airplane. Other times I was the formation lead in my own jet. Either way, my career really had come full circle.

Yet as important to me as the Navy's continued loyalty was the fact that those final two years afforded me a luxury I had rarely experienced in my career to that point: predictability. For the most part, I knew from day to day, week to week, and month to month what my schedule would look like. That predictability let me do things on a regular basis, which doesn't happen when you're deployed at sea for many months at a time. Among those things was surfing.

Generally speaking, the Navy is an incredibly fast-paced organization, and in turn one that demands a fast-paced lifestyle. It doesn't really afford its people the chance to sit back and reflect. Surfing does. In spending a good part of my free time these past two years on a surfboard, I was able to think through the many things I learned in the military and in life over the course of my career. The product of those reflections, obviously, is this book.

At the risk of being reductive, I think the primary lesson I've taken from all my experiences in the Navy came when COVID-19 struck the *Theodore Roosevelt* and I was forced to stand up for what I believed in. At that moment, all the other lessons I had learned throughout my career came to a head and helped me to decide what kind of leader I wanted to be. It's easy enough to tout the merits of relationships while you're sipping espresso or playing softball. But to put your own ass on the line to defend the people that form those relationships, well—as I said earlier—that's where true character can be forged.

Sometimes you have to make decisions that contradict what your boss wants you to do: damn the consequences and be true to yourself and your beliefs. Your decision might be completely wrong. But I would argue that even if it turns out you're wrong, it's better to do what you believe is right than second-guess yourself into indecision. Not everyone gets tested in that way in life, but if and when the time comes—when things are NKR and you are comfortable with your moral beliefs—there is no better feeling than taking a stand for what you know to be right.

While doing that cost me my opportunity to complete my command of the *Theodore Roosevelt*, I wouldn't change a thing about the experience, and I remain loyal to the Navy— particularly naval aviation—even now. That's why Mary and I were honored to attend the commissioning ceremony of our middle son, Sean, on the USS *Constitution*, aka "Old Ironsides," a wooden-hulled frigate that's still a part of the Navy and is the world's oldest ship still afloat.

That day, May 26, 2022—almost thirty years to the day that I was commissioned on May 27, 1992—would be the last day I ever wore a uniform as an active-service member in the US Navy. Four days later, I would officially retire. Yet as Sean saluted me—his first as an ensign in the Navy to a senior officer—and I saluted him back on the pier beside that storied vessel—my last as a captain—I knew the Navy would remain a part of our family business for many more years to come.

So when people ask me if I'm bitter about how the Navy treated me in the wake of the COVID-19 outbreak on the *Theodore Roosevelt*, the answer is a resounding no. When you take a stand, you have to accept that others may not agree with your decision. But that doesn't mean you have to hold it against an organization you've been part of for more than thirty years.

So as I look back on that time, I recognize how extremely lucky I've been. I chose a path thirty-four years ago that I couldn't see clearly, nor truly understand at the time. It ended up being a path that I have found both rewarding and challenging, and much more fulfilling than I had ever hoped for as an eighteen-year-old kid from Northern California. It afforded me a career of adventure, travel, and excitement and, most importantly, introduced me to the people who would better my life forever.

In the meantime, all branches of the military remain a family business for hundreds of thousands of others who currently serve, brave volunteers who stand ready and on watch all across the globe . . . in the air, at sea, and ashore. While they, like me, may have joined for adventure and rewards, they put themselves in harm's way primarily because of a steadfast belief in something bigger than themselves. Never forget them, or what they stand for. Our nation, and our way of life, are better because of them.

So, I say the same thing to them—and to you—as I did at the end of my announcements on both the *Theodore Roosevelt* and the *Blue Ridge*, words I will strive to live by beyond my time in the Navy:

Keep your head on a swivel,
your eye on a shipmate,
and be ready for the fight when the day comes.

Acknowledgments

It's been said that if you see a turtle on top of a fence post, you know it didn't get there by itself. So after a thirty-year military career, there are many folks that this particular turtle on a fence post would like to thank for helping me get here today and write this book.

First, to my beautiful wife, Mary. They say in life one of the most important decisions you'll ever make is whom you choose to marry. Choose correctly, and that single decision will eclipse whatever else you do and lead to a life of happiness. In my case, I got that decision right. Thanks for your love, inspiration, editorial assistance, and for being the cornerstone of our family, no matter where life took us.

My boys, Connor, Sean, and Ian, you keep me young at heart and always excited to learn new things. Thanks for joining me on hikes, backpacking trips, science experiments, surfing sessions, movie binges, New Year's Eve PT sessions, baseball games, and all the adventures we've had around the world. And to our dog Charlie, in case she can read and we just don't know it yet: you're a good dog.

My wonderful parents, Bob and Gina, you have provided more love and support than any one kid ever deserves, and obviously it was at the expense of my sisters (just kidding!). Thanks for your genuine encouragement, no matter what adventures I chose to embark on.

My sister Becky, who recently left us after a long battle with cancer. I've been blessed to be influenced by tough women my entire life, from my trailblazing grandmothers to my mom, aunts, sisters, and my wife . . . as well as the female fighter pilots whom I flew with in combat. But Becky might have been the toughest of them all, for the simple reason that despite the challenges, the treatments, and the huge inconveniences that cancer caused her over the last couple years of her life, she never stopped fighting for what she believed in and the people she loved.

My sisters Bridget and Betsy; their husbands, Todd and Ryan; Becky's husband, Tim; and all my nieces and nephews (Melina, Maggie, Molly, Sophie, **Hayley**, Summer, and Cal). As your big brother, brother-in-law, and uncle, I couldn't have asked for a more supportive family. And of course a special shoutout to Betsy, who was a brilliant assistant editor, confidant, and business partner throughout the entire process of writing this book.

My in-laws, aunts and uncles, relatives, godparents, neighbors, and extended family from Santa Rosa and beyond, I appreciate all the support you have given us over the years, starting way back when I was a little kid still figuring out the world in Northern California. You remain a huge positive influence in my life.

My high school friends from Santa Rosa, classmates from the Naval Academy (Jeff, Mark, and Brett), and shipmates from every duty station I've been assigned to from the day I was commissioned until today—you remained loyal friends from the start and were never afraid to speak up publicly on my behalf. Thank you.

To the "Holy Cow Ladies!" (Pat, Sandra, and Kristin) who provided incredible support and research over the last two years keeping track of world and Navy events better than most collegiate historians could ever hope to do.

I would never have embarked on this journey were it not for the encouragement of my high-school friend Max, who assured me I could write a book about my career in the Navy that would be entertaining, positive, and worth reading. My book agent, Byrd Leavell, provided great assistance from the start, then continued to provide sage advice throughout the process. To the entire team at Simon & Schuster Atria Books—my editor, Peter Borland; his assistant, Sean deLone; as well as the rest of the team (Karlyn Hixson, Lisa Sciambra, Shida Carr, and Morgan Hoit)—I am very thankful for your input, guidance, and advice.

And to my cowriter, confidant, and great friend Mike Vlessides. You made writing this book an incredibly enjoyable experience. I've always said that "written out is thought out" and you definitely helped me think through all the stories and lessons from my career that I wanted to tell . . . in a way worth sharing. I consider you a true shipmate and thank you for all your assistance along the way. Thanks as well to your lovely wife, Caroline, for her willingness to provide us immediate and honest feedback on every chapter as soon as we were done. I look forward to seeing a couple baseball games with you and eventually teaching you how to *really* surf.

And finally, to all the Sailors and friends I've had the honor to serve with, as well as those that remain on watch throughout the world today. You continue to make our nation proud, and every day live up to the motto of *Non sibi sed patriae*: Not to self but for country.

Thank you.

*A portion of the book's profits will go to
nonprofit organizations focused on supporting
our nation's service members and veterans.
To learn more about these and several other
outstanding charitable organizations please
visit www.surfwhenyoucan.com.*